Twentieth-Century Influences on Twenty-First-Century Policing

Continued Lessons of Police Reform

Jonathon A. Cooper

LEXINGTON BOOKS
Lanham • Boulder • New York • London

Published by Lexington Books
An imprint of The Rowman & Littlefield Publishing Group, Inc.
4501 Forbes Boulevard, Suite 200, Lanham, Maryland 20706
www.rowman.com

Unit A, Whitacre Mews, 26-34 Stannary Street, London SE11 4AB

British Library Cataloguing in Publication Information Available

Library of Congress Cataloging-in-Publication Data
Library of Congress Cataloging-in-Publication Data Available
ISBN 978-0-7391-8904-7 (cloth : alk. paper) -- ISBN 978-0-7391-8905-4 (electronic)
ISBN 978-1-4985-1593-1 (pbc: alk. paper)

∞ ™ The paper used in this publication meets the minimum requirements of American
National Standard for Information Sciences Permanence of Paper for Printed Library
Materials, ANSI/NISO Z39.48-1992.

Printed in the United States of America

I dedicate this book to my daughter, Zoë Caitlin. I love you.

Contents

Chapter One

Introduction

This is a book about policing in the 1950s, 60s, and 70s—and what it means for policing in the 21st century. Such an opening sentence may not come off all that compelling, but it should. In terms of policing science, these three decades—especially the two most recent—were arguably the heyday for police theorizing. As Jack Greene (2013) put it: "This 'foundational era' of police research produced much of what has been tested subsequently. Initial observational studies of the police from the 1950s and throughout the 1970s produced much of what is still known about the internal workings of the police" (p. 9). Certainly we have had and continue to have our fair share of policing theorists since then, most notably Robert Langworthy (1986), John Crank (2003), Pamela Jackson (1989), Thomas Bernard and Robin Engel (2001), and David Klinger (1997). But today's policing researchers tend to be drawn toward seemingly atheoretical evaluation studies (Cooper & Worrall, 2012; Greene, 2013) or the integration of criminological theory (e.g., Wolfe & Piquero, 2011; Chappell & Piquero, 2004). As I have indicated elsewhere (Cooper & Worrall, 2012), there is merit to this integrative approach. But there's a reason why such good and interesting theories about policing behavior and organization were developed by the likes of John Van Maanen (1974), Peter Manning (1978), Herman Goldstein (1979), Donald Black (1976), Jerome Skolnick (1966), Egon Bittner (1967), David Bordua (1967), Albert Reiss (1971), Michael Banton (1964), James Q. Wilson (1968), William Westley (1970), and Arthur Niederhoffer (1969), to name just a few, at the tail end of what scholars now consider the end-days for the professional policing era: events in the 1950s, 60s, and 70s created tectonic shifts in how the police in the United States operated. It was an exciting era that demanded explanation—an era with ramifications for policing that still direct police policy and operations today.

This was especially true in terms of the relationship between the police and society. The way policing functioned in the 50s, 60s, and on into the 70s, coupled with a number of pivotal events, created a tangible malaise between police and civilians—including between the police and the courts.

These events included, among others: the due process revolution, which changed *how* police were to do their job; social science research that called into question that efficacy of *how* the police were doing their job under the professional model; and race riots against police activity, which were, in large part, the result of poor police-minority community relations. These (and other) events demonstrated two things about police: that their relationship with the citizenry was poor, and that the traditional way of doing police work was ineffective. A volatile combination that would be the prelude to a number of changes in American policing that now shape contemporary law enforcement behavior and organization. This book outlines these events, explores their implications for the relationship between society and the police, and suggests that a knowledge of these changes is imperative to understanding trends in contemporary policing as well as the direction policing needs to take.

Twentieth-Century Influences on Twenty-First Century Policing is organized in the following manner. Chapter 2 provides readers with an overview of general American policing history, including the British roots of American policing; slave patrols in the South; early American policing and its development into what scholars now call the "Political Era," including a discussion of the catalyst of immigration; the professional model, including a discussion of the professionalization movement and the work of August Vollmer, and the impact of professional policing on the relationship between society and the police. In addition, chapter 2 will discuss how scholars now classify contemporary policing and the transitions policing underwent throughout the 80s and 90s (and that continue today).

Chapter 3 discusses what has become known as the "due process revolution," a phrase used to describe the activity of the United States Supreme Court under chief justice Earl Warren. Throughout Warren's tenure, the Supreme Court ruled on a number of cases that impacted not only police behavior, but also how society saw the police, and how the police saw themselves in relation to society and the government. This discussion is extended in chapter 4, which focuses on two issues relating to civil rights: race riots and the changing role of women in policing. Considerable attention is given to the race riots that broke out around the United States in the 1960s, and the President's Commission on Law Enforcement and Administration of Justice's response to these race riots with its publication *The Challenge of Crime in a Free Society*. Chapter 5 concludes the civil rights discussion by considering the diametric of American government and policing in the 50s and 60s and, although waning, in the 70s. Specifically, while government was heavily liberal in its approach to crime and justice, particularly in the late 50s and throughout the 60s, policing, both as an occupation and in terms of individual police officers, remained (and remains) conservative.

Taken together, the first four chapters should demonstrate that the events that will have been thus far covered in the book served to increase feelings of isolation by both the police and society in terms of "the other side." Such feelings broke down any meaningful communication between the police and society, and thus the ability of police to effectively work with communities to fight and prevent crime. The next few chapters discuss events that called into question the effectiveness of the crime-control tactics the police traditionally employed. This starts with an overview, in chapter 6, of other intellectual changes that were occurring in criminal justice generally, and explores their impact on American policing. More specifically, it relies on the work of the American Bar Foundation and its "discovery" of discretion in criminal justice agencies, as well as the work of the President's Crime Commission and its publication *The Challenge of Crime in a Free Society* in creating an integrated systems approach to criminal justice. This was the first time the police, courts, and corrections were understood to be related to one another in a coherent system. Among other things, scholars learned that police were not always enforcing the law, and police learned that when they did enforce the law their efforts were often countermanded by the behavior of the courts.

Chapter 7 reviews seminal empirical research undertaken in the 1970s about the effectiveness of various police functions, including: the Kansas City Preventive Patrol Experiment (Kelling et al., 1974); research on rapid response time (Pate et al., 1976); and the effectiveness of detectives in solving crime (Greenwood & Petersilia, 1975), among others. These studies put into question the effectiveness of the professional policing model and its traditional reactive tactics, suggesting that perhaps police were not the professional crime fighters Vollmer had envisioned them to be. Such findings were underscored with an increasing crime rate coupled with corrupt police behavior, covered in chapter 8. Prior to the 1970s, crime in the United States had been increasing concomitantly with population and immigration. This changed in the 1970s, as the nation saw an enormous uptick in crime across the board that could not be explained by population growth alone. As with the events described in chapter 7, the increasing crime rate called into question the effectiveness of traditional policing tactics and strategies. In addition, this chapter will highlight the Knapp Commission's findings on police corruption in the New York City Police Department.

The final chapter, Chapter 9, serves as the denouement of the previous 7 chapters (2-8). The events covered in these chapters demonstrate that police and society (including the government and other criminal justice agencies) were not seeing eye-to-eye, and that the traditional manner of doing police work was no longer seen as viable. This situation came to a head at the end of the 1970s and at the start of the 1980s when demands for police reform took center stage. A discussion of the importance of community, on total quality management, and problem-oriented policing follows, as well as a discussion on the importance of innovation, technology, and the scientific method for policing for reducing and preventing crime. For each of these topics, it is demonstrated how they "fix" a "problem" that came to light in the 50s, 60s, and 70s. In addition, things that have *not* changed and *why* they have not changed are also discussed, including: the professional model, seeing police as crime fighters, and the traditional police mandate to protect the innocent and catch the villain.

At the end of Chapter 9, two innovative and contemporary policing practices will be discussed in light of how each responds to the concerns of the 50s, 60s, and 70s: the SMART policing initiative and Project Safe Neighborhoods. These are promising endeavors that represent a shift in how the police go about fighting crime. In many respects, they are a combination of both conservative and liberal tactics, and employ a multiagency paradigm and cutting edge social scientific research. Policing in the 21st century is changing—and it is changing due in large part to important events at the latter half of the 20th century.

As policing becomes more technologically savvy and scientific in its approach to fighting crime (for example, the SMART Policing Initiative, COMPSTAT, and problem oriented approaches such as Project Safe Neighborhoods, all of which are discussed in more detail in chapter 9) at a time when governments are being faced with austerity (Sindall & Sturgis, 2013; Brogdon & Ellison, 2013), it is important to reconsider how policing got to the point it is so that, as police and governments move forward, constitutional guarantees are protected, communication with citizens remain viable and salient, and crime prevention becomes an empirical reality rather than a nonoperational ideal (cf. DiIulio, 1993). This book, then, is not a history of policing, *per se*, so much as an analysis of historical events pertinent to policing through the lenses of the sociological imagination.

I wish to acknowledge the assistance and inspiration of the following individuals, without whom this book would never have been written. For inspiration, I thank Andrew Giacomazzi from Boise State University, Michael White and Charles Katz from Arizona State University, John Worrall from University of Texas, Dallas, and Robert Kane from Drexel University. For assistance, I thank the army of graduate students at Indiana University of Pennsylvania who provided feedback and proofreading work, including: Kyle Ward, Kweilin Pikciunas, Robert Stallings, Lori Wiester, Darla Darno, Paul Hawkins, Myunghee You, and Lyndsey Smathers. I especially thank the essential book hounding and research work done by Cassie Stroman. I thank all the good folks at Lexington Books who made this book possible, and the supportive environment created by my colleagues at IUP that facilitated its writing.

Chapter Two

A Primer on the History of American Policing

This chapter provides an overview of American policing history. Such an overview is important because the concept, structure, and function of the American police did not develop in a vacuum. In order to understand the events of the 1950s, 60s, and 70s, and their impact on policing, it is necessary to consider key historical events that lead up to these decades. For example: without an understanding of colonial (and post-colonial) southern slave patrols or the relationship between the creation of the police in New England and the increased immigration of Catholics from Europe in the 19th century, it is impossible to fully appreciate the racially charged environment in which the police of the 1960s worked. Just as this book contends that events in the 50s, 60s, and 70s presaged changes to police form and function, so too did the events prior to these decades set the stage for the radical shifts in society and law enforcement that the remainder of this book details.

To this end, I cover the following events in this chapter. First, I consider the two primary sources of American policing: the Anglo-Saxon model under Sir Robert Peel and the southern slave patrols of antebellum America. I then discuss the events leading up to the creation of a formalized police force in the United States, and review the two periods of American policing history conventionally called the Political Era and the Professional Era. I briefly consider several of the consequences of the Professional Era that not only swept in a new era of policing history but also radically changed the relationship between the police and society. As these events are the focus of this book, I treat them cursorily here. I conclude this chapter with a short examination of how policing scholars have labeled the era—or eras—following the Professional Policing Era.

BRITISH ROOTS OF AMERICAN POLICING

For the most part, a state sanctioned police force, independent from the military and the citizenry, did not exist in the British Isles until the early 1800s. Prior to this, policing was informal and sporadic, and emanated from family units. British policing before the 1800s can be divided into two time periods: before and after the Statute of Winchester, which was written down in 1285 (Johnson, 1981). Prior to 1285, and under Saxon rule, families were responsible for the law-abiding behavior of their members: when one broke the law, it was their responsibility to apprehend him and present him for punishment. Additionally, when someone was suspected of a crime, a "hue and cry" was raised; male family members, typically those twelve years of age and up, were obligated to respond to the hue and cry and give chase. After the Norman Conquest of 1066, this system of kin policing developed into the more formalized, but still family-centered, frankpledge system (Uchida, 2005). Under the frankpledge system, families were organized into groups of tens called *tithes*, which were organized into groups of one hundred called *hundreds*, which were in turn organized into *shires*. Within a hundred, a *constable* administered justice; within a shire, a *shire reeve* supervised the constables. According to the frankpledge system, families were not only responsible for their own members' behavior and responding to the hue and cry, but also detained suspects for trial and convicts for punishment, and testified in court.

The frankpledge system was modified by the Statute of Winchester in 1285 (Johnson, 1981). This Statute, and the resulting system of justice administration, laid the groundwork for both British and American policing. For Great Britain, the Statute of Winchester provided the legal precedence that Sir Robert Peel would need in the 1820s for a state sanctioned police force. For the United States, the Statute set up a system of justice administration that would cross the Atlantic and form the basic framework of American colonial and post-colonial policing. The Statute of Winchester, among other things, formalized the role of constables and placed more power in their hands. According to Uchida (2005), such a move was necessary because the frankpledge system was disintegrating, due to a substantial lack of oversight by the Crown. In its place, a new system of watchmen was introduced. Under the "watch and ward" system, the constable would assign male citizens to patrol city streets during the night. Patrols were divided into what would (much) later be called *beats* (Reppetto, 2010).

Even though the Statute of Winchester and the frankpledge systems were more formal than the kin policing of Saxon England, none of these efforts really reflect the idea of a formalized, state sanctioned police force as we understand it today. Both systems, while overseen by a constable, sheriff (the eventual portmanteau of the *shire reeve*), and later justices of the peace, relied on the informal participation of citizens. This, in itself, had a number of unintended consequences: constables, who were often drawn from the ranks of the lesser lords, typically hated the work and hired it out to less-than-qualified individuals; and watchmen also resented their appointments and would rarely carry them out to completion (Johnson, 1981; Reppetto, 2010). Despite their flaws, however, these systems managed to work due in large part to the nature of medieval society.

Economically, medieval society was pre-industrial and agrarian, and relied on a barter economy more related to feudalism than the capitalism that would emerge in the 17th and 18th centuries (Polanyi, 2001). As will be pointed out shortly, British industrialization changed everything. Theoretically, medieval Britain is best conceptualized by Tönnies's (2002 [1957]) *Gemeinschaft* or Durkheim's (1997 [1933]) idea of mechanical solidarity. In the English translation of Tönnies's *Gemeinschaft und Gesellschaft*, *Gemeinschaft* is rendered (when it is translated at all) as *community*. *Gemeinschaft* describes a social aggregate built around personal relationships and common values. A formalized system of justice administration, such as a state sanctioned police force, is unnecessary because behavior is regulated informally through socialization and shaming.

What interested Durkheim was the question of what made a society a society—that is, what bound its members to the social aggregate. His term for this, translated from the French, was *solidarity*. In his *De La Division Du Travail Social*, Durkheim formulated two solidarities: mechanical and organic. He described almost all pre-industrial societies as possessing a mechanical solidarity. A society whose solidarity was mechanical was one where relationships with other members of the society were interpersonal rather than professional. For example, when someone was hired to do a job they were hired largely because of who they were in relation to the hirer, rather than their formal occupation. These sorts of relationships are called *first order relationships*, and are often based on kinship and marriage. In a society characterized by mechanical solidarity, crime is less prevalent because there is an absence of anonymity. In addition, because of this lack of anonymity, criminals are readily apprehended. Finally, because there is typically a consensus on values, there is no need for a police force to mediate between disputing parties. In communities characterized by *Gemeinschaft* and a mechanical solidarity the informal systems of British policing during the Middle Ages essentially worked. Two important events happened during the 1700s in Great Britain, however, that would radically alter first British and then American policing irrevocably: the Industrial Revolution and the Enlightenment.

THE INDUSTRIAL REVOLUTION AND THE ENLIGHTENMENT

The system of British policing under the Statute of Winchester began to fall apart in the late 1700s (Uchida, 2005). In part, this was because of the laziness and ineptitude of the constables and nightwatchmen. As is so often the case even today, however, there was more at work than simple police ineffectiveness. Johnson (1981) accurately sums up this disintegration thusly:

> During the eighteenth century, policing under the ancient system of constables and watchmen finally collapsed. Widespread incompetence among peace officers contributed to this breakdown, but the more fundamental reasons for its downfall arose from a massive social and economic transformation of English society. (p. 11)

Two of the most influential "massive social and economic transformations" were the Industrial Revolution, which began in Great Britain in the late 1700s (Polanyi, 2001) and that period of intellectualism known as the Age of Enlightenment, which affected both European and colonial American thinking during the 17th and 18th century.

The Industrial Revolution was characterized by a number of interrelated factors. Economically, communities began moving away from the traditional barter and feudal systems of medieval Europe to one based on capital and labor. This was due in no small part to the industrialization of commodities and goods. One consequence of this industrialization was a shift from agrarianism to factories. Because factories were built near urban city centers, this shift in turn created a large migration from the rural, agrarian English country-side to its urban, industrial cities. Large cities, such as London and Birmingham, and port cities, like Liverpool, became inundated with migrants. As a result, their populations grew rapidly. London, for example, grew to almost a million residents between 1700 and 1800 (Johnson, 1981). Most of these migrants were poor, and remained poor despite the long hours they were required to work in the factories. In addition, for many families, both the father and the mother worked, leaving a relatively large population of unattended (and in many cases, orphaned or abandoned) children to roam the streets (Uchida, 2005).

Theoretically, these changes represented a shift from Tönnies's *Gemeinschaft* to *Gesellschaft* and from a solidarity that was mechanical to what Durkheim would call organic. *Gesellschaft* is usually translated as *society*, but this is a very inexact translation. It is better understood as a social aggregate characterized by impersonal interactions and values that are codified and formally common to all citizens of that social aggregate. Similarly, a society based on organic solidarity is one where relationships are of a second order:

where we hire people to do a job because that *is* what they do. In such a society, people specialize in occupations, and hire out their labor. Because people no longer ask their friends and family to help them, but instead hire someone whom they may not know, laws flourish so that when one person hires another person's labor, both parties fulfill their obligations of payment and product. Along with those laws, a system to administer and adjudicate the laws must follow to provide them with some teeth. Stated in another way, the large populations and anonymity associated with societies characterized by organic solidarity require a complex legal setup. But the system of law enforcement set up under the Statute of Winchester, and most visibly represented by the nightwatchmen, simply could not keep up with these rapid social changes (Johnson, 1981). The system responsible for administering and adjudicating the law had no teeth.

In retrospect, then, it should be no surprise that crime, unrest, and turmoil accompanied these social and economic changes (Reppetto, 2010). London's upper class not only disliked the migrants but also saw them as little more than vermin: dangerous and unwanted. Factory workers and their families were also dissatisfied with the way things were going in England, and expressed their discontent with riots about food, wages, poor public sanitation, and general working conditions (Hall & Hay, 1980). In addition, street crime was increasing in urban cities (Uchida, 2005). Such conditions were combined with an unhealthy dose of national paranoia. According to Reppetto (2010),

> The eighteenth century was also a time of political unrest characterized by great fear of Jacobites, Papists, Irish rebels, and French spies who were often imagined to be behind various riots. Thus crime and disorder tended to be viewed as threats to the existing social and political system. (p. 10)

Despite these conditions, the British parliament simply did not care. The only thing that local constables could do was hire more watchmen. This, unsurprisingly, did not work (Johnson, 1981). Some people turned to the private sector. One such entrepreneurial group were the "thief takers," lead by the notorious Jonathan Wylde. Their job was to find victims' possessions after they were stolen. This resulted in no small amount of corruption, however, with many thief takers working in collusion with gangs of thieves and sharing in the profits. Others who could afford private bodyguards did, but this was very limited. Meanwhile, the great urban cities of Britain continued to deteriorate into chaos. As one contemporary, Daniel Defoe, in a pamphlet he wrote about crime in London in 1730, wrote:

> The Whole City...is alarm'd and uneasy: Wickedness has got such a Head, and the Robbers and Insolence secure within their own Walls, or safe even in passing their Streets, but are robbed, insulted, and abused, even at their own

Doors...The Citizens...are oppressed by Rapin and Violence; Hell seems to have let loose Troops of human Devils upon them; and such Mischiefs are done...as never were practised here before (at least not to such a degree) and which, if suffered to go on, will call for Armies, not Magistrates, to suppress. (Quoted in Skolnick & Fyfe, 1993, p. 67)

The unrest culminated in 1780 with the Gordon Riots. Protesting against the weakening restrictions against Catholics in Great Britain, an estimated fifty thousand persons rioted through London. Nearly three hundred persons were killed by the British Army, and over four hundred were arrested. Defoe's statement, penned fifty years earlier, was vindicated. The Gordon Riots sparked a national debate about police reform in Great Britain, but almost to no effect. This, despite continual confrontations between British Protestants and Irish Catholics. As Walker (1998) has suggested, this was in part due to governmental inertia and in part to a fear of government expansiveness and power. This latter fear seemed especially vindicated *by* the Gordon Riots, where the national army was responsible for so many citizen deaths, and which was sparked by a government action that went against popular senti-ment. Although there were national police models in embryo in both France and what would later become Germany, they came with their own baggage of government corruption and misuse that the English wanted to avoid. Despite the unrest, increase in crime, and lack of governmental ability to do anything about it, England would need something else before they would submit to a state sanctioned police force. Even then, their "submission" was at first reluc-tant and hesitant, filled with trepidation and wariness.

That "something else" was Enlightenment thinking. Enlightenment think-ing is characterized by a number of ideas, including using the scientific method in all manner of scholarly disciplines besides the natural sciences and extending them to public policy; a focus on humanity, individualism, and the relationship between the individual to the state; and the importance of ration-ality—that *things* need to make sense. *All* things were scrutinized under the lens of the Enlightenment for an evaluation of their rationalness and humane-ness. Under such a microscope, 18th century British justice failed. For exam-ple, British reformers were repulsed by the volume of capital crimes under common law (around two hundred) after reading the Italian Enlightenment criminal justice reformer Cesare Beccaria's *Of Crimes and Punishment.* They were equally moved by the political writings of the Genevan Jean-Jacques Rousseau and their own John Locke, Thomas Hobbes, and Jeremy Bentham (all of whom would influence the framers of the American Consti-tution), who wrote extensively of the social contract, and the idea that the state had an obligation under the social contract to protect the well-being of the body politic.

Two British criminal justice reformers would set the stage for Sir Robert Peel who, in the early 1800s, would push legislation through Parliament to create the first British state sanctioned municipal police force. One was the novelist and British marshall, Henry Fielding. Fielding began the process of significantly decreasing the number of capital offenses in Britain. He did so under the Enlightenment-influenced thinking that the punishment was too harsh for too many crimes to have any effect; rather, he argued, the government should focus on the root causes of crime, which, according to Fielding, were social in nature. Additionally, Fielding founded the Bow Street Runners with his half-brother, John Fielding. The Bow Street Runners were highly effective and highly moral thief takers that did the same business as Jonathan Wylde, but without the collusive relationships. Their Runners were composed of constables hired under Henry in his capacity as marshall (Johnson, 1981). The Fieldings's Bow Street Runners demonstrated that the government could have an effective and non-corrupt police force.

Perhaps most important for Peel, however, would be the work of Patrick Colquhoun. Colquhoun, like Fielding, was influenced by Enlightenment thinking. He argued that policing should not be communal, as it effectively was under the Statute of Winchester, but should instead be the responsibility of the state (Johnson, 1981). He was given the opportunity to put his political philosophy to work when he was tasked with reducing the cargo theft that was occurring regularly on the Thames River. His answer was a small police force which would patrol the river front. Initially this police force was private; but after its apparent success, it was placed under public control in 1800, and renamed the Marine Police Force, which would itself later become part of Peel's Metropolitan Police (Harris, 2002). Indeed, Colquhoun's writings, including *A Treatise on the Commerce of the Police and the River Thames*, *A Treatise on the Functions and Duties of a Constable*, and *A Treatise on the Police of the Metropolis*, along with his own legislation, penned with Jeremy Bentham, to create the Marine Police Force, were all seminal to Peel's own policing model. It is to the creation of Peel's Metropolitan Police that we now turn.

SIR ROBERT'S PEEL'S "BOBBIES"

While there remains some scholarly debate about which reformer is the father of modern policing—Colquhoun or Peel—this debate bears little relevance for our current purposes. The fact of the matter is that *both* mattered. Without Colquhoun, there is very little possibility that Peel's efforts would have been successful. And it was Peel who would be able, eventually, to push the legislation known as the Metropolitan Police Act of 1829 through Parliament. (And if we are to be utterly historically honest, the Glasgow Police Act of 1800 is an even more likely candidate for the title of the first state sanctioned municipal police force in the Western world.) Peel's Metropolitan Police Act is important and relevant because it became the model for both British and American police agencies, and outlined a democratic policing ethos that resonates today. However, Peel had to contend with a host of concerns about a state sanctioned police force that were held by both the government and the governed.

These concerns have been outlined above. To briefly recapitulate, the British were worried about expanding the power of the state, and about the state abusing policing powers. There was ample precedent for this sort of abuse, both in terms of an unfortunate history of the British army being set against its own citizenry, and in terms of contemporary abuses being committed by the Parisian police (Reppetto, 2010). Despite these concerns, it was obvious that *something* had to be done to stem the tide of rioting, disorder, and crime. As British Home Secretary, Peel was tasked with figuring out what that *something* was to be. Peel believed that a preventive police force was the answer, but he was up against a bulwark of public and political wariness against this idea. Rather, the preferred response was to change the law—and changes did happen, but to essentially no effect (Johnson, 1981). Aided by the real and perceived disorder wracking urban England, Peel succeeded in finally passing his Act through Parliament thanks to several astute strategies.

First was how the Act itself was written. Peel narrowed the jurisdiction of his preventive police to the greater London area (hence, the *Metropolitan* Police Act). This curtailed the government's reach with their new police. Second, he carefully crafted the new government office to respond to Parliament's concerns. For example, he made the goal of the police to prevent crime through a visible presence through patrol. Their success would be measured not by how often they *arrested people*, but by the absence of criminal activity. A focus on prevention meant, in theory at least, that the opportunity for abuse and corruption was attenuated (Walker, 1998). (This idea of *police-as-visible-deterrent-through-patrol* remains a hallmark of both British and American policing.) Additionally, while the police were to be controlled by the government—that is, not by the private sector—they would *not* be under the aegis of the military. This reduced the concern over military abuses and over privatized corruption, as had been witnessed under Jonathan Wylde's thief takers. Importantly, however, the police would be organized along paramilitary lines, specifically, after the British navy. In both the 18th and 19th centuries, the Royal British Navy was *the* pinnacle of order, tradition, honor, and exemplary behavior. Not only did the British police adopt the hierarchical organization of the navy (and along with this structure, military titles were also adopted), they also adopted uniforms. The uniforms of the police would not be red, like the navy's, though; they would instead be blue. This move was subtle, but a stroke of genius: by how they dressed the new police evoked the order and discipline of the Royal Navy, without suggesting that they *were*, in fact, the navy (or army, for that matter). To further quell concerns about whom the police served, Peel made it clear that the police were to be accountable not just to the Home Secretary, but to the citizens under their watch. As such, officers were given badges with identifying numbers that were to be visible at all times, and were taught to be patient and to resort to violence only as a final resort.

Once the Metropolitan Police Act passed through Parliament, Peel installed two police commissioners, who were also carefully chosen. From the military, he chose Colonel Charles Rowan; and from the private sector, he chose the barrister Richard Mayne. By doing so, Peel made manifest the two facets of the Metropolitan Police: a paramilitary structure and discipline in tandem with a respect for the rule of law and the desire to serve (Johnson, 1981). Under Rowan and Mayne, Peel's campaign to alleviate the public's concern over his new "Bobbies" continued. Police were chosen from the working class and usually from the communities that they would later serve (among other innovations, Peel divided the London metropolitan area into *beats* that officers would patrol and for which they would be accountable; as I have discussed extensively in another work—*In Search of Police Legitimacy: Territoriality, Isomorphism, and Changes in Policing Practices*—and as Rubinstein first really articulated in 1973 in *City Police*, the territorial nature of both police organization and behavior remains a defining characteristic of Western policing). The thought was that by removing anonymity, and by drawing on a sense of community, the desire and opportunities for corrupt and abusive behavior would be diminished. Additionally, his Bobbies received training and endured a probationary period of employment. Initially, Peel, Rowan, and Mayne's high standards were unmet by the police officers who were hired, and the public remained skeptical for some time afterward. Eventually, however, the Metropolitan Police would emerge as a model for local, municipal policing that would change how societies thought of public, formal social control. When cities in the *New* England states in America were looking for public answers to their own problems of crime and disorder, it was primarily to the Peelian model that they turned (Walker, 1998).

THE TWO ORIGINS OF AMERICAN POLICING

Walker (1998) has noted that the "London Metropolitan Police...provided the principal model for the new American police" (p. 53). The Peelian model of policing would travel across the Atlantic around the mid-1800s. Before that, policing in America looked very similar to 12th century British policing: nightwatches, constables, sheriff's, and citizen patrols. In addition, there

were several vigilante groups composed of the elite of society whose goal
was to apprehend lawbreakers and, often, meet out justice (Lane, 1980). For
the same reasons that this setup could not endure in England, it was doomed
in America. As Walker (1998) has also noted, the "sequence of events in
England paralleled that in the United States" (p. 53). Like Great Britain, this
informal, communal system of policing fell apart as the colonies, and later
the United States, shifted from a mechanical solidarity and a *Gemeinschaft*
society to an organic solidarity and a *Gesellschaft* society. The more industri-
alized the United States became, as farmers moved into urban centers and
social relationships broke down into economic transactions, laws flourished
as did those who broke the laws. In addition, economic-based riots from the
poor against the rich and the government, although not necessarily becoming
commonplace, were on the rise. As with Britain, crime and the image of a
dangerous underclass prompted several cities to reconsider the need for the
police. Initially, a handful of cities—including Philadelphia, Boston, New
York, and St. Louis—experimented with paid day- and nightwatch programs
(Fosdick, 1969). In the South, a form of vigilante policing was already established prior to the New England experiments. Known as slave patrols, their
job was to apprehend and return runaway slaves (Wadman & Allison, 2004).
These two disparate styles of policing, the slave patrols of the South and the
Peelian model of the North, would ultimately evolve into modern American
policing.

Throughout New England and the Mid-Atlantic, and in some cases the
Midwest, once it became apparent that the dual day- and nightwatch system
was not adequate, municipalities began modeling a publicly sanctioned police force after the Peelian Bobbies. Cities like Boston and Philadelphia
adopted and adapted Peel's model, including uniforms and a paramilitary
structure, and a focus on preventive patrol (Walker, 1998). But there were
some significant differences between the two systems, owing largely to how
the United States was set up politically compared to Great Britain. In England, the Metropolitan police were centralized at the federal level under the
Crown. In the northeast United States, cities took center stage in the development of police departments (Walker, 1977). This pattern of localized—that
is, decentralized—police forces was because of at least two things. First, in
the United States, as a democracy, "local solutions to local problems" was
very much in vogue until the early 20th century. Second, the very nature of
American democracy, that is, republicanism, is one of federalism, with codified and enforced distinctions between the various levels of government.
Such a political milieu meant that policing across the United States was not
immediately uniform, either in their duties or behavior. However, it did not
take long for police departments to start acting and looking alike (Walker,
1998). As will be discussed below, this political atmosphere was extremely

detrimental to the initial relationship between the society and the police, and would presage many of the problems encountered in the 1950s and 1960s.

Similar problems would evolve out of the slave patrol system of the South. Slave patrols were established in the South for two purposes: to capture and punish runaway slaves, and to prevent white abolitionists from assisting runaway slaves. They were, for the most part, well-organized vigilante groups who would seek out escaped slaves and those who assisted them, and either return them to the plantation owner or, in some cases, punish them upon capture. These were not necessarily voluntary patrols: most slave-owning landholders were required to be a part of the patrols, and to take the job seriously (Wadman & Allison, 2004). This meant that the problems experienced in England with lazy nightwatchmen, who often pawned their job off on equally lazy substitutes, were not necessarily an issue in the South. Rather, slave patrols were brutal and effective. The institution of slave patrols also set the stage for the poor relations between police and Black communities that would come to a head in the 1960s in Chicago (among other cities). Essentially, one origin of American policing can be found in the creation of a police force designed explicitly to subjugate an entire group of people. That background will remain part of the relationship between Black communities and the police well after the passage of the 13th and 14th amendments.

The causes and implications of these changes in American policing are manifold and directly relevant to this book's thesis. In the South, one of the major contributors to creating a police system was a minority population, African slaves; in the North, it was not only Black Americans, but also the presence of new, immigrant populations. In this case, immigrants from Ireland, Italy, and Eastern Europe, who shared a religious heritage that was an affront to American Protestantism: they were Catholics. They were believed not only to teach "anti-American" values, but to live them: laziness, intemperance, and idolatry. Additionally, it was largely the Industrial Revolution that brought these populations to the United States and into the cities. This resulted in the same sort of food riots as witnessed in England. Mob violence was also popular as a means to enforce public morality and ethnic and racist (against immigrants and against freed slaves) sentiment throughout the northeast (Walker, 1977). Further, although the idea of localized policing sounded good, it would result in some negative consequences for the relationship between the police and society, eventually forcing the federal government to step in (throughout the 1950s, 60s, and 70s), both directly, through court cases handed down by the United States Supreme Court, and indirectly through monies, training, and college programs and education. Because of the decentralized structure of American politics and hence policing, the new police forces were tied to their municipal governments in a way alien to their British counterpart. This so-called "Political Era" of American policing is discussed below, along with its consequences and eventual development into the "Professional Era" under August Vollmer and J. Edgar Hoover. Walker (1998) best summarizes the policing that was evolving in the mid-1800s thusly: "The result was a hopelessly unprofessional, inefficient, and incompetent style of policing" (p. 54). So many of the events discussed in this section will resonate later in American history, with important ramifications for the police, especially in the decades with which this book is most concerned.

AMERICAN POLICING ERAS: POLITICS AND PROFESSIONALISM

While scholars may differ as to where policing went, paradigmatically, after the 1970s, most agree that prior to the 1970s, American policing can be divided into two eras: the Political Era (roughly 1830–1900) and the Professional Era (roughly 1900–1960) (Walker & Katz, 2011). These eras are defined according to the behavior and function of the police, the organization of police agencies, and the relationship between the police and society. As indicated above, the police of the Political Era reflected their English counterparts—to a lesser or greater degree, depending on which police function or organizational characteristic one is focusing on. Ultimately, American policing was its own creature, and would develop in growth spurts punctuated by social crises that would lead to radical changes.

THE POLITICAL ERA

Although scholars refer to the period of roughly 1830–1900 in American policing as the *political* era, its defining characteristic would have to be *corruption*. Corruption in American policing was both widespread and part of the larger political landscape of 19th century urban America (Uchida, 2005). This was due in no small part to the decentralized nature of American politics. Johnson (1981), for example, notes the following irony: "Politics affected the organization and the behavior of the police in both England and America. The difference in political influence became apparent, however, in the effect which politics had. In England, politics contributed to the success of the new police; in America politics severely hindered police effectiveness" (p. 32). There were no standards to which police were held, no means of accountability, and no consensus on what, exactly, the police were supposed to be doing. This opened up the possibility for those in power to maintain their elite status and political positions by using the police as tools (Walker, 1977). And from all the available evidence we have, it was a possibility that many municipal politicians availed themselves of—from aldermen to mayors (Lane, 1980).

In all fairness and historical accuracy, not all was contrived in policing during this era. Indeed, when it came to the community, the police were quite service oriented: maintaining homeless shelters, soup kitchens, and even orphanages (Lane, 1980). Additionally, even though one of the reasons police were introduced in New England and the Mid-Atlantic was related to a fear of immigrants from Ireland, Italy, and other non-Protestant European nations, it's also true that as these ethnic groups began to assimilate into the culture of the United States, they were in turn hired as police officers. In both of these regions of America, the police were being used to break up protests, often violently, on behalf of the corporate owners who were part of the city's political machine. This situation became rather complex, however, because many of the workers who were protesting were newly immigrated ethnic minorities from Europe, including Ireland, Italy, and Eastern Europe. As each ethnic group assimilated into the American population, they would often be given policing jobs. In such a situation, they would then often *help* organized labor when protests were being run by those of their own ethnic group (Walker, 1998).

It was common during the policing era for police jobs to be doled out to friends and political allies in a system known as patronage (Walker, 1998). Additionally, promotion within a police department often came with a price tag of what even today would be considered an exorbitant price *without* taking inflation into consideration (some promotions cost upward of $15,000) (Uchida, 2005). Similar to their British counterparts, the first American police officers were *a priori* unpopular with the public. Patronage and their involvement with the political machine *de jour* only heightened the public's dislike with the new police forces, which were popping up in every American city seemingly overnight (Monkkonen, 1981). Often, this dislike manifested in violence against the police—against which the police responded with violence (Johnson, 1981). This cycle of "disrespect leads to violence leads to disrespect" is to be a recurring theme in American policing history that yet haunts American law enforcement today, and which would ultimately come to a head in the 1960s. In the 19th century, this cycle was caught up in the myriad of police problems associated with political machines that would boil over in the late 1800s.

During the latter half of the 1800s, a group of reformers turned their attention to a number of matters that they perceived as problems in American society and government. These reformers, the Progressives, were mostly composed of middle-class White Protestants who were concerned with a number of social and political ills, including the administration of government (Platt, 1977; Walker, 1977). Although not all of their efforts were aimed at police directly (some were—and these mostly failed), their actions would reverberate to law enforcement agencies. Their efforts culminated in the passage of the Pendleton Act of 1883, an act designed explicitly to deal with the nepotism endemic to the Grant administration (White, 2007). The Pendleton Act required civil service standards for the hiring and termination of all public employees. While it applied initially only to the federal government, it soon spread across state and local governments throughout the United States. The effect on the police would eventually be dramatic: it was the first step toward police reform that would include both standards and accountability. It would take more than the Pendleton Act and its children to change the police, however; while the Act might have freed police from the patronage system of the 19th century's political machines, the police were still left in a mandate-less limbo. This was to change. The development of the International Association of Chiefs of Police (IACP) in the 1890s would be the first indication that more concerted reform was on its way (Lane, 1980). The IACP was part of what is known as the professionalization movement in American government—and it was a movement that would sweep police reform thanks to a number of catalytic police leaders, most notably August Vollmer.

THE PROFESSIONAL ERA

Walker opens his 1977 book with this powerful statement: "Professionalization was an attack upon the pervasive influence of partisan politics on American policing in the nineteenth century" (p. 3). Politics have never been completely removed from American policing (Strecher, 1991); nor, constitutionally, could they. It is for this reason that the Progressive's initial efforts to fully divorce the police from politics, beyond the influence of the Pendleton Act, failed (Uchida, 2005). What the Progressives, did, however, was pave the way for other police reforms. It was in fact because of the political nature of policing that it was amenable to being reformed: like almost all American government entities in the early 1900s, police departments were overwhelmed by the professionalization movement that was impacting government at all levels. Still, it would take nearly three decades for professionalization to fully take hold of American policing (Johnson, 1981). Indeed, according to Walker (1977), professionalization *never* took hold of American policing. Rather, *bureaucratization* did. In other words, policing carried with it the *form* of professionalization (the bureaucracy) but not the function. Whatever the case may be, the early 20th century would shape policing nationwide into an institutionalized organization that even today we recognize.

Professionalization carried with it two components, one organizational and the other ideological. At the heart of the latter was crime fighting (Johnson, 1981). Monkkonen (1981) refers to this as the narrowing of the police function. Whereas in previous decades the police were created and pitted against a "dangerous underclass" of immigrants and rural migrants, now they were focused on chasing criminals. Although Vollmer would try to reinvigorate a social service role for the police such as we saw in the Political Era (less the nepotism), this would come into conflict with the role of professional crime fighters—and in this conflict, social services would lose (Walker, 1977). Instead, the police adopted a mandate of "efficient, apolitical, and professional enforcement of the law" (Manning, 1978, p. 8). Part of being a "professional," in any capacity, was adjusting one's occupational frame of reference: one's *job* was more than an *occupation*, it was a *vocation*. In a Weberian sense, your job is not what you do, it's who you are. For the police, this mandate defined not just what they did, but who they were—as police officers and as human beings: they were the police, professional crime fighters laden with the responsibility to protect the innocent and catch the villain. This is an obvious about-face from the political and corrupt activity that generally described the police in the 1800s.

In the vanguard of this professional policing mandate and image was the still relatively new Federal Bureau of Investigation (established in 1908), under the leadership of J. Edgar Hoover, whose long tenure began in 1924. The leading role of the FBI was not an accident—rather, it was by Hoover's design (Walker, 1977). The FBI touted—some might say flaunted—both its training and technological expertise. Part of this process would be the acquisition of the IACP's nationwide Uniform Crime Reporting system, which acquisition itself would have important ramifications for how the success of police were judged throughout the Professional Era, which would in turn greatly affect police organization and behavior. In addition, the FBI regularly advertised its field agents' exploits in catching notorious criminals, particularly those involved in organized crime. Under Hoover's politically and media savvy eyes, the FBI honed the concept of "public enemy number one." Their professional image—clean-cut and well trained men of the law, fluent in cutting edge technology and criminalistics, and patriotic crime fighters— would find its way into almost every local municipal and county police agency throughout the United States (Johnson, 1981).

This new mandate and ideology of professional and apolitical crime fighting were to be expressed by the organizational changes that professionalism brought. At the center of these changes was August Vollmer, who cut his teeth at police reform by spearheading the Wickersham Commission's report on the use and consequences of the infamous "third degree" during police interrogations. Walker (1977) compartmentalizes these changes into seven domains. First, organization and procedures were streamlined. Following Weber's idea of an ideal bureaucracy, police agencies became pyramidal and hierarchical, with decision making centralized at the top in the hands of the chief. Second, again following Weber's bureaucratic ideals, operations needed to be *rational*, that is, measurable. For the police, this manifested in terms of *numbers*, or, as Skolnick and Fyfe (1993) would later call it, the *numbers game*. Although this "game" would include a variety of numbers, including calls for service, time on the beat, summonses, and revenue and expenditures, the primary means of quantifying success for the police in America would be arrest and clearance. Arrest and clearance rates, codified in the Uniform Crime Reports, would be used to hold police agencies to account again and again throughout American history, often with less than positive implications for the relationship between society and the police.

Third, after the Wickersham's Commission's damning exposé of police brutality in the form of the third degree, and after several decades of political corruption, American police agencies were sensitive to their public image. To this end, they cleaned up that image. For the first time, uniforms in American policing became standard. In addition, and fourth, agencies tried to raise the quality of their police officers. Formal, extensive, and standardized training became the norm. Vollmer took this one step further and developed the first baccalaureate degree in criminology at Berkeley in 1916. Indeed, the relationship between the police and police scholars has been close since the dawn of the Professional Era, as many university professors were hired to teach the first police academy classes. In part, this was due to the new academic field of criminology, and the fifth characteristic of the professionalism movement in policing: the ready adoption of new and sometimes exciting technology, such as the mass-produced automobile and two-way radio.

While all of the changes that professionalism brought to policing were in some manner in response to the corruption endemic to policing during the Political Era, the final two characteristics were in direct response to this corruption. First, all reasonable measures were taken to insulate the police from politics. Police unions and civil service exams for both hiring and promotion were seen as ways to protect line officers—and the brass—from the meddling of city hall. And finally, standards of operations, in tandem with new paperwork, were created as a way not just to hold officers accountable and to maintain records (a special obsession of bureaucracies), but to literally reduce the discretion available to line officers. The idea was that by reducing discretion, an agency could reduce the opportunity for personal corruption, such as bribe-taking and extortion. For the first twenty or thirty years of the Professional Era, many police agencies believed that this last ideal was in smooth operation—that when an officer had probable cause, he would act to make a lawful arrest. It would not be until the 1950s, after the research into the operations of the criminal justice system (which at that time was not yet perceived *as* a system) by the American Bar Association, that police agencies would "wake up" and realize that line officers still wielded incredible discretion in the execution of their duties while they were on the street—standard operating procedures and paperwork be damned (Walker, 1998). Despite this hiccup, the professionalization of policing would utterly revamp the police occupation—both conceptually and operationally.

UNINTENDED CONSEQUENCES OF PROFESSIONALIZATION

The police professionalization movement had several unintended consequences when it came to the relationship between the police and society. With their *über*-focus on crime fighting, and the service aspect of policing left by the wayside, citizens were seen through one of two lenses: Either you were a crook or you were a witness. (Van Maanen [1978] offers a few more typologies than this, so perhaps it's more correct to say that citizens were only seen as *useful* if they fit into one of these two caricatures.) With the destruction of the socially empathetic character of policing, police adopted a cool and aloof—almost scientific—approach to the execution of their duties, which had been narrowed to crime fighting. The 1950s radio and television drama *Dragnet* captured the spirit of this disinterested persona with Sergeant Joe Friday's famous catch-phrase, "Just the facts, ma'am." The divide between the police and society was beginning to widen.

This new distance between the police and the public was compounded and complicated by two factors, both related to technology. First, the patrol car meant that police were no longer interacting face-to-face as often with citizens—and when they were acting face-to-face, it was rarely for pleasant, neighborly reasons. In addition, it meant that they could cover more ground on patrol, which, while enhancing their geographic knowledge of their beats, reduced their familiarity with the people who lived within their jurisdiction. Yet at the same time the police were isolating themselves from the public— both ideologically *and* literally—they were now becoming involved in the most intimate elements of citizen's lives. This situation was made possible because of the two-way radio, which could be used to send officers on patrol anywhere in the city, and the new ability, thanks to personal telephones, to phone the police headquarters directly to report crime. The police welcomed and encouraged the use of the telephone for just this reason (Walker, 1998). But the result of these "calls for service" was not always to report crime but to ask the police to settle disputes or to solve problems—sometimes serious but sometimes trivial. The police became, in the words of Egon Bittner (1970), the people whom citizens called upon when something "that-ought-not-to-be-happening-now-and-about-which-somebody-had-better-do-something-now" (p. 30). Yet the police only had one tool to "officially" handle any scenario that came their way: the enforcement of the law, which typically translated into arrest. Often, this was *not* the outcome for which those who called upon the police were looking.

The widening divide between the police and society was not something that police were able to keep up with, for a number of reasons. Most pertinently, they could do little to attenuate this divide because they were simply not set up to adapt to external forces. By definition, bureaucracies—the organizational tool by which professionalism operated—do not change: they are closed organizations that rely on an assumption that the environment is stable so that routine activities can function correctly. Society, however, is anything but stable—and while it advanced in one direction, American policing staunchly placed its heels into the dirt and refused to even recognize where society was trying to take them. By the late 1950s, and certainly by the 1960s, this had developed into a solid "us-versus-them" attitude. Perhaps nowhere is this inability to respond to social changes more demonstrable than in Chicago in the 1960s, where August Vollmer's reforming protégé and the chief of the police, O. W. Wilson, failed to read the racially charged winds and adapt accordingly. Despite Wilson's success at reducing corruption in the Wichita City, Kansas, police department in the 1920s and 1930s (Bopp, 1977), he failed to meaningful respond to the boiling hatred against the Chicago Police Department in the 1960s. His failure would, in part, be responsible for the race riots that plagued Chicago in the late 1960s (Walker, 1998). These unintended consequences set the stage for the tectonic changes in both American police and society in the 50s, 60s and 70s.

THE NEED FOR CHANGE

The social isolation that was coming to define the relationship between the police and society, in tandem with four emerging social and political patterns directly involving the police, portended another reformation, this time of the Professional Era and its assumptions. First, the increasing social distance between the police and citizens, coupled with the us-versus-them animosity that the police were now harboring, soon broke down communication between the police and the neighborhoods that they ostensibly served. This was to have an especial effect on *minority* communities. Recall that for African Americans and to a large degree Latinos and other ethnic and religious minority groups, their relationship with the police, historically, was one of systemic oppression. Indeed, for African Americans, this relationship predated the Professional and Political eras, starting with the Slave Patrols. African American communities did not, however, fare any better in the North under the activities of the political machine-controlled police of the Political Era. Such was the case first under Black Codes and then under Jim Crow, and always under a taint of prejudice. Now, in the Professional Era, African Americans were either being ignored or harassed. And in the 1960s, on the heels of *Brown v. Board of Education* (1954), yet before the institutionalization of *Brown* had been realized everywhere in the United States, riots broke out around the nation.

These riots brought just how bad minority relations were with the police—and how poorly that message was being received by municipal police agencies—to the attention of the nation, particularly to the federal government. In the late 1960s, following the Chicago riots, the federal government created the Kerner Commission and the President's Commission on Law Enforcement and the Administration of Justice. The latter, in their 1967 document *The Challenge of Crime in a Free Society*, planted the blame squarely on the shoulders of the police for their part in instigating the riots. They noted that the poor relations with minority communities was something the police had created, that it had been a major cause of the riots, and that it was something that the police needed to fix (Walker, 1998).

These reports came at about the same time as social scientists became very interested in what police did. American universities (and the Federal government) produced a host of research demonstrating that police behavior under the professionalism model—behavior held sacrosanct by police departments as part of their mandate and vocation—was not effective at "fighting crime." Indeed, by way of the work of Angell (1971), the very notion that the primary role of police *was* to fight crime came under scrutiny. Police staples like random patrol, detective work, and even the deterrent effect of arrest all came under the unforgiving lens of the social scientific method. The results called into question the very foundation of 20th century policing.

At the same time, the United States Supreme Court was seemingly handing down ruling after ruling labeling a number of professional police tactics as *unconstitutional*. This era in American jurisprudence was to have such an impact on how police went about enforcing the law that it would be labeled the Due Process Revolution. At the center of these Supreme Court cases was Chief Justice Earl Warren, who, depending on how one feels about the rulings generated under his tenure, was either one of the most famous or most infamous Supreme Court Chief Justices to ever sit on the bench (Graham, 1970). Police strategies such as custodial interrogation, stop-and-frisk, and other activities orbiting the twin concepts of *search* and *seizure* were suddenly endowed with strict constitutional guidelines. Police felt as if the Supreme Court were handcuffing their ability to do their jobs, and expressed their feelings vocally during this period (Walker, 1998). Between the social scientist's research findings, riots against the police and the concomitant blaming of the police by the federal government, and the opinions of the Supreme Court, the police across the nation felt as if their "us-versus-them" attitude was not only justified, but that they were on the losing side of that battle. It was a time when police felt they were disliked, untrusted, and alone. These feelings would cement their strong *esprit de corp* and further enforce the "blue code of silence," patterns which would themselves create problems that continue to plague American police agencies (Walker, 2005).

Perhaps most concerning for the police was the irrefutable evidence that *crime was going up*. As if the social science research was not enough to demonstrate their efforts did very little to reduce crime, a national pattern of increasing violent crime, which would take off in the 1970s (and, of course, explode in the 1980s), was just too much. If they were supposed to be the professional crime fighters, they were failing. In short: the professional model had failed the police and had failed society. It was time for a serious change. All of these patterns heralded a number of changes, each of which were in response to the problems that the professional model created. The police would need to figure out new ways to improve their image, to be effective, and to be efficient.

Policing scholars since the 1980s have included other eras following the professional. This pattern began with Kelling and Moore (1988), who argued for a "community problem-solving era". By this terminology, Kelling and Moore meant that not only were police engaging in problem oriented tactics *á la* Herman Goldstein (1979), but that police were refocusing on broadening the scope of their professional mandate. Part of this process, according to Kelling and Moore, was to employ community oriented policing as a new framework. Not everyone has agreed with this taxonomy. For example, Strecher (1991) challenges the notion that police is or even could be moving toward a community era of policing based on community oriented policing. Rather, he suggests that the community era of policing may simply be an academic artifact—the product of the cherry-picked experiments and studies of criminal justicians. He notes that:

> If community policing is largely a reified concept at this time, a creature of the academic literature rather than a defined, measurable and widespread approach among the 17,000 local policing agencies, a reason for the academic explosion on its behalf should be found. The energy being expended in producing community-policing literature may be greater than the energy of community policing being expended on the streets of America's cities. (p.7)

Uchida (2005) has pointed out that community policing has no single definition. As such, it is difficult to use its name as the new policing era's title. Similarly, Walker and Katz (2011) do not even bother to conceptualize policing history into specific eras. Rather, they talk (fruitfully) about policing in terms of its development in the 19th century, the beginning of professionalism in the early 20th century, the radical changes in police administration in the mid-20th century, and what they subhead as "New Developments in Policing, 1970–2000" (p. 47). Under this heading they discuss community policing, but alongside several *other* policing innovations. This scholarly conversation is somewhat beyond the scope of this book. It is worthwhile to note, even if in passing, however, that the claim that the era of policing since the 1970s can best be described as a *community* era is qualifiedly incorrect.

If by "community" we mean a renewed focus on the relationship between the community and the police, and all that that might imply, then perhaps there is some truth to this, as the remainder of this book will demonstrate. But if by "community" we mean an era of policing characterized by *community oriented policing* then the case for a community era cannot be sustained. There is no indication that community policing has ever operationally taken hold across the United States, at least not as originally articulated by Trojanowicz and Bucqueroux (1990). Rather, all evidence points to a piecemeal or sandbox approach to community policing, where agencies borrow certain strategies or tactics here and there (Worrall & Zhao, 2003; Zhao, He, & Lovrich, 2003). Indeed, as Thurman, Zhao, & Giacomazzi (2001) note in their community oriented policing textbook: "Asking the question, Does community policing work? means asking about specific program activities, objectives, and goals" (p. 239). Yet community policing is not supposed to be a suite of programs: it's supposed to be a complete renovation of the philosophy of policing, along with law enforcement strategies and tactics (Roberg, Novak, Cordner, & Smith, 2012).

If not community policing, then what? If we must insist on an era, instead of going the direction of Walker and Katz (2011), I submit that if there is one characteristic that has emerged within American policing over the last thirty or forty years—albeit relatively slowly and with more variation than what we have seen in previous eras—it would focus on the idea of *crime prevention through the scientific method.* This focus includes the increasing and increasingly innovative use of technology in ways that not even Vollmer could envision. I will revisit the use of technology and the scientific method in 21st century policing in Chapter 9, as it has become a hallmark response to the lament that "police can do very little to reduce crime" (Herbert, 2001, p. 449)

The chapters that follow focus on the challenges to the police that professionalism presented, and the ways in which police have responded to them. In addition, I consider what these challenges and responses mean for policing in the 21st century. In brief, my thesis is the following: Events in the 1950s, 1960s, and 1970s have shaped policing in the 21st century. Just as we saw colonial policing problems presage the creation of policing in the Political Era, and as the problems characteristic of Political Era policing were, in large part, the catalyst for the professional reforms, so too did the events of the three decades that are the focus of this book—and these events *must* be understood in the context of professional police reforms—explain many of the innovations we've seen in policing since the 1970s.

Chapter Three

The Due Process Revolution and the Warren Court

In this chapter, I consider the impact of the so-called "due process revolution," a period of Supreme Court activity that lasted roughly ten years in the 1950s and 1960s. The impact of this period cannot be understated; indeed, although we have a better idea of how it has affected American justice administration than we did while it was happening, we are still disentangling all of its effects and implications, as well as the way it has shaped our modern conception of American justice. The effects of the due process revolution were both empirical and normative: not only did it change *how* police worked, it changed how we thought police *ought* to work. Also, not only did it increase the malaise between civilians and police officers, it endowed those same civilians with a knowledge of their rights, as well as demonstrable proof that they could stand up for these rights against government intrusion at the hands of the police.

Two court cases in particular are important to consider: *Mapp v. Ohio* and *Miranda v. Arizona.* Both of these cases greatly expanded the application of the federal exclusionary rule to the state level. The net effect was that police were held accountable to the Bill of Rights, while simultaneously giving them the impression that their crime fighting powers were being curtailed. Among other things, this lead to an increase in the us-versus-them attitude already endemic among police officers during the professional era. At the same time, the case of *Terry v. Ohio* greatly expanded the power of the police to interfere in the routine activities of civilians, lowering the threshold for some stops and searches. This paradox created an explosive concoction that would itself have great effects at the later ends of the 1960s.

This chapter first considers the Supreme Court and the man at the center of the due process revolution, Earl Warren. An unexpected champion of civil rights and due process, Warren became both a hero and villain to the American public and criminal justice system during his tenure, while radically transforming the very ethos of both in terms of justice and its administration. Then, I consider the *Mapp, Miranda*, and *Terry* cases, covering their rulings and context, and evaluating both their empirical and normative impacts. Although their tangible effects are rather few and far between, the degree to which they have and continue to influence the relationship between the police and society is penetrative.

CHIEF JUSTICE EARL WARREN AND HIS COURT

The Due Process Revolution was so called because, as Fred Graham (1970) notes in his book of the same name,

> ...what the Court did was to refine the meaning of the due process requirement of the Constitution, which until then required only that states observe "fundamental fairness" in criminal matters. The Warren Court changed the due process requirement to demand absolute compliance by state and local police with the key provisions of the Bill of Rights. For a process that was accomplished in less than a decade, this could properly be called a "due process revolution." (p. 6)

As this quote and the subheading above indicate, the Chief Justice of the United States Supreme Court in the 1950s and 1960s, Earl Warren, was at the heart of this revolution. Scholars tend to agree that, along with John Marshall, Earl Warren was one of the most important justices to sit in the Chief's chair. Both Marshall and Warren earned this title because of the impact that their courts had: Marshall's for expanding the Supreme Court's power, and Warren's for incorporating most of the Bill of Rights to the states (Newton, 2006).

Prior to his nomination to the Supreme Court by President Dwight Eisenhower, Warren was already familiar both with politics and with the American court system. While Warren did work a short stint in a small private legal practice, most of his professional life was spent as a public servant, first as a district attorney for Alameda County, California, and then as attorney general for the state of California. Additionally, Warren was serving his third term as governor of California when the Eisenhower appointment came down (Horwitz, 1998). As Chief Justice, and despite his background in law and public service, Warren was not known as an intellectual powerhouse. Instead, his talents were more personal in nature. He had a knack for forging majorities and consensus within the Court by force of both his charisma and passion. In general, Warren was well-liked, and despite several smear campaigns against him, legitimate complaints were both limited and lacking (Newton, 2006).

Many of the cases for which the Warren court would issue writs of certiorari would involve police behavior, including evidence collection (e.g., *Mapp v. Ohio* in 1961), stop and frisk (e.g., *Terry v. Ohio* in 1968), and custodial interrogation (e.g., *Miranda v. Arizona* in 1966). Warren's influence extended beyond policing, of course, to include seminal cases in desegregation (e.g., *Brown v. Board of Education* in 1954), privacy (e.g., *Griswold v. Connecticut* in 1965), in voting district reapportionment (e.g., *Reynolds v. Sims* in 1964), and in court processes, as well (e.g., *Gideon v. Wainwright* in 1963). Additionally, he worked to essentially discredit the political witch hunts of the McCarthy era (e.g. *Watkins v. United States* in 1957), and spearheaded the commission charged with investigating the assassination of President John F. Kennedy. The impacts of the Warren Court were far reaching, indeed; for our purposes, and for the sake of brevity, we will focus on those cases most intimately and famously connected to policing behavior. Almost all of the cases tried during Warren's tenure, however, would receive significant criticism from nearly all sides of the political aisle (and continue to receive much criticism today).

Some of the Court's most divisive cases—*Pennsylvania* v. *Nelson* (1956), which dealt with state-lead anti-communist programs, and *Brown* v. *Board of Education* (1954) lead to great ire against the Court in general, and Earl Warren specifically. *Nelson*, especially, lead to a campaign to impeach Warren on grounds of treason (Newton, 2006). Although reactions against the Court's policing/due process cases did not reach that fervor, Warren's efforts in this milieu did not exactly score him friendships among police—a historic irony given his work as a district attorney in California. Lead by Warren, the Court's efforts to hold local police strictly accountable to the standards of the Bill of Rights were perceived as "handcuffing" the police from doing their job and letting bad people go free on nonsense legal technicalities that had no attachment to the reality of crime in America. As we will explore below, these perceptions were unfounded, and in many cases, the intended consequences of the due process rulings were never realized (Graham, 1970). Nevertheless, two points about the Warren Court are important to consider.

First, although the due process revolution did not have all of the dire nor the meritorious consequences its critics or authors intended, it did succeed in stabilizing the American criminal justice system and making it more fair to defendants and criminal justice actors (Graham, 1970). Second, whatever its intended or actual consequences, conservative police officers saw the due process revolution as palpable proof of their us-versus-them attitude: not only was the public against them, so too was the government. Rather than allowing them to go about doing their job of effectively and efficiently fighting crime, the Supreme Court was perceived to be rendering their job as inefficient as possible, with the potential consequence of rendering it ineffective as well. The social isolation of the police, as created by the characteristics of the Professional Era, was given cohesion by the Warren Court's due process revolution. I elaborate on these points in the following sections.

FOUNDATIONAL COURT CASES

The Warren Court's due process revolution covered a number of domains. In the following paragraphs, I review the rulings for three that have had the most widespread impact and popular awareness as related to the police: the exclusionary rule, stop and frisk, and the *Miranda* rights. Each of these domains would influence how both the police and society—and, more generally, the criminal justice system—framed American law enforcement. Although their practical impact may have been minimal (as discussed in the proceeding section), this does not mean that their rulings were trivial. As the latter half of this chapter will point out, quite the contrary.

The Exclusionary Rule

Broadly speaking, the *exclusionary rule* dictates that whenever law enforcement gathers incriminating evidence outside the boundaries of due process, that evidence must be omitted from trial. Even more broadly speaking, *due process* refers to the guidelines outlined by the Constitution, specifically by the Bill of Rights and the 14th Amendment. The exclusionary rule's corollary, the Fruit of the Poisonous Tree Doctrine, is even more punitive in its ramifications for not following due process; this doctrine states that, not only must the evidence that was illegally obtained be omitted from trial, so too must all evidence that resulted from the initial illegal discovery. These legal doctrines were not first enunciated by the Warren Court. Rather, their precedence was wrought out earlier in the 20th century, most famously in the federal case *Weeks* v. *United States* (1914). As was the case for many of the rulings handed down by the Warren Court, the exclusionary rule was not novel jurisprudence so much as novel application: through the 14th Amendment, the Warren Court incorporated the exclusionary rule to the states and, by extension, municipal governments and their law enforcement agencies.

In *Mapp v. Ohio* (1961), the Warren Court did just that. The exclusionary rule is based on the 4th Amendment's protection against unlawful searches and seizures (at the hands of the government). As a general rule, police require both probable cause *and* a warrant "particularly describing the place to be searched, and the persons or things to be seized" to actually search and seize someone's person and property. According to the Supreme Court of the United States, the Cleveland police failed to do that in their search of Mapp's home and during the subsequent arrest. What the police did do was present Mapp with a piece of paper that they called a search warrant. After a physical struggle for the "search warrant," Mapp was detained while the police searched her home for materials related to a bombing suspect. The police were unable to recover any relevant bombing evidence, but they did find evidence of "obscene material" (a subject that had also come before the Warren court in *Roth v. United States* in 1957), for which Mapp was convicted.

Mapp appealed her conviction, arguing that the exclusionary rule, as articulated in *Weeks v. United States*, applied to the states as equally as it did to the federal government, via the due process clause of the 14th Amendment, which reads: "...nor shall any State deprive any person of life, liberty, or property, without due process of law..." The Supreme Court granted writ, heard oral arguments in March of 1961, and handed down a ruling a few months later, agreeing with Mapp and reversing her conviction: "Since the Fourth Amendment's right of privacy has been declared enforceable against the States through the Due Process Clause of the Fourteenth, it is enforceable against them by the same sanction of exclusion as is used against the Federal Government." The "same sanction of exclusion" refers directly to *Weeks'* exclusionary rule: such evidence was to be *excluded* from trial.

The word *sanctioned* used by Justice Clark in writing the court's 6–3 majority opinion denotes a *punishment* for police misbehavior. As Justice Clark noted: "Were it otherwise, then just as without the Weeks rule the assurance against unreasonable federal searches and seizures would be 'a form of words.'" In other words, the exclusionary rule, while *designed* to protect the rights of the defendant from the awesome coercive power of the state ("...without that rule the freedom from state invasions of privacy would be so ephemeral and so neatly severed from its conceptual nexus with the freedom from all brutish means of coercive evidence as not to merit this Court's high regard as a freedom 'implicit in the concept of ordered liberty'"), was *applied* to punish the state—as made manifest by law enforcement agents and agencies—for ignoring due process. Such implication would weigh heavily against the relationship of the police with the courts and the public.

Miranda Rights

Unlike *Mapp*, *Miranda v. Arizona* (1966) did not represent the application of a previous federal case to the states via the 14th Amendment. Instead, it represented the extension of a previous incorporation of the 4th Amendment. Thirty years earlier, in *Brown v. Mississippi* (1936), the Supreme Court had ruled that violence could not be used to coerce a confession out of a defendant. They based their ruling on the 14th Amendment's due process clause. *Miranda* essentially extended this protection to other forms of coercion, with the proviso that, like the exclusionary rule, any deviation from affording such protection would place evidence (specifically, confessional evidence) in jeopardy. The Warren Court went one important step further in *Miranda*, literally requiring the police to delineate these protections verbally to suspects, and to only proceed with a custodial interrogation once the suspect had intelligently and willingly waived the protections. As with the *Terry* case discussed below, *Miranda* has required dozens of cases to specify exactly when and how it does and does not apply. The core of the case's outcome, however, remains intact: suspects have certain protections against self-incrimination, *inter alia*, and the police must make them aware of these protections before proceeding.

The *Miranda* case made its way up to the United States Supreme Court on two constitutional grounds: the right to legal representation and the right to protection from self-incrimination, drawn from the 6th and 5th Amendments, respectively, and incorporated via the 14th Amendment. Neither of these were afforded to Miranda, who was accused of kidnapping and sexual assault and interrogated for two hours, after which he orally confessed and then signed a written confession. Because his rights were never outlined to him, Miranda's lawyer argued that his confession should be omitted from trial. Both the trial court and the Arizona State Supreme Court disagreed. On a 5–4 decision, however, the United States Supreme Court ruled in favor of Miranda. In so doing, the Court articulated five specific rights that suspects must be made aware of whenever in custodial interrogation:

The person in custody must, prior to interrogation, be clearly informed that he has the right to remain silent, and that anything he says will be used against him in court; he must be clearly informed that he has the right to consult with a lawyer and to have the lawyer with him during interrogation, and that, if he is indigent, a lawyer will be appointed to represent him. And in addition:

> If the individual indicates in any manner, at any time prior to or during questioning, that he wishes to remain silent, the interrogation must cease ... If the individual states that he wants an attorney, the interrogation must cease until an attorney is present. At that time, the individual must have an opportunity to confer with the attorney and to have him present during any subsequent questioning.

This case was a long time coming, and it represented a growing malaise with the nature of police interrogations. The general sentiment was that police were coercing confessions, if not in a violent manner then in a decidedly unconstitutional manner. This was the Court's not-too-subtle shot over the bow that such behavior—acceptable under the professional model—would no longer be tolerated. The response from the police was a shattered feeling that their efforts at fighting crime were unequivocally and purposely being stymied by the Supreme Court. In large part because of *Mapp* and *Miranda*, the police accused the Court of handcuffing law enforcement and precluding them from accomplishing their professional mandate (Graham, 1970).

Stop and Frisk

Unlike the other topics discussed in this section (the *Mapp* and *Miranda* cases), the Warren Court's rulings on the police practice of stop and frisk, set forth in another Cleveland, Ohio, case, *Terry v. Ohio* (1968), did *not* limit the power of the police. On the contrary, they expanded their coercive power. Although the message was different, the implications for the relationship between society and the police were no less important. In some respects, the ramifications of the *Terry* case were the most important among the due process cases, if for no other reason than its impact is still felt today in a very real, on-the-street way. For example, *Terry v. Ohio* provides the legal rationale for the zero-tolerance policing practiced by the New York City Police Department, among other agencies, which is currently subject to serious legal dispute. As with *Mapp*, *Terry v. Ohio* concerned the application of the 4th Amendment to the states, but both the jurisprudence behind *Terry* and the Supreme Court's opinion in *Terry* departed radically from the spirit of *Mapp*.

Terry involved a veteran police officer observing the dubious behavior of three individuals whom the cop rightly suspected of "casing" a store. The officer asked them their names; they responded with mumbles. The officer then responded by patting one of them down and finding a pistol. Concerned for his safety, the officer then frisked the other two men, eventually uncovering another weapon. Two of the men were charged and convicted of illegally carrying concealed weapons. When they appealed on grounds that the state lacked probable cause for such a stop and search, two appeals courts upheld the trial court's verdict, and the Ohio State Supreme Court dismissed the case from their docket. The Supreme Court, however, granted writ and ultimately upheld the lower court's verdict. In so doing, the 8–1 majority, which included one justice concurring, agreed with the lower courts that there were two events to consider, the stop and the frisk. As long as the former was non-intrusive and relatively short in duration, and based on what the court would define as *reasonable suspicion*, it did not need probable cause. Further, if an officer had *reasonable suspicion* that a suspect may have a weapon, and that his person or that of others may be in danger, he could conduct a pat-down of the suspect's outer clothing *sans* warrant.

This ruling and its specificity are important. In discussing *Terry v. Ohio*, Hemmens, Worrall, and Thompson (2004) state that "much police activity does not reach the level of intrusion that occurs when a search or seizure is carried out...If probable cause were required under such circumstances, there would be very little the police could do in terms of investigating suspicious activity" (p. 45). But this behavior could only be taken so far: the stop must be short and non-intrusive, and the frisk must only be of the outer clothing, for weapons, and for the officer's or others' safety. Like *Mapp* and other search and seizure cases, the rationale behind *Terry* comes from the 4th Amendment: "The right of the people to be secure in their persons, houses, papers, and effects, against unreasonable searches and seizures, shall not be violated..." In this case, the search and seizure—that is, the stop and frisk—is not deemed to be *un*reasonable.

Key to understanding *Terry*, then, and its implications for police behavior (and later, for the relationship between police and society), is the legal concept *reasonable suspicion*. As the majority noted in their opinion:

> Where a reasonably prudent officer is warranted in the circumstances of a given case in believing that his safety or that of others is endangered, he may make a reasonable search for weapons of the person believed by him to be armed and dangerous, regardless of whether he has probable cause to arrest that individual for a crime or the absolute certainty that the individual is armed.

The Court went on to define how reasonable suspicion was to be developed: "The reasonableness of any particular search and seizure must be assessed in light of the particular circumstances against the standard of whether a man of reasonable caution is warranted in believing that the action taken was appropriate." Like so many Supreme Court tests, this one is vague by design to allow for maximal application. Hemmens and colleagues (2004), in an attempt to clarify its ambiguity, admit that "[t]here is no clear definition of 'reasonable suspicion,' just as there is no clear definition of probable cause." They then cite a later United States Supreme Court case (*United States v. Sokolow* in 1989, under the Rehnquist Court) and offer the following definition of *reasonable suspicion*: "As a level of justification lying below probable cause, then, reasonable suspicion is 'considerably less proof of wrongdoing by a preponderance of evidence' (*United States v. Sokolow*, 1989), but more than an unparticularized hunch" (p. 45). That there were over twenty years between *Terry* and *Sokolow* is a telling hint at the sort of wide latitude that *Terry v. Ohio* would—and to a large degree continues to—give police officers in their street-level activity. Indeed, Hemmens, Worrall, and Thompson (2004) conclude their discussion of *Terry v. Ohio* thusly: "This decision, handed down by the often vilified 'liberal' Warren Court, was actually a major victory for police officers" (p. 47).

THE EMPIRICAL IMPACT OF THE DUE PROCESS REVOLUTION

One of the major social concerns with the Warren Court's rulings in the areas of the exclusionary rule and the 5th Amendment was that criminals would be let off, wholesale, based on technicalities. Subsequently, it was feared that crime, especially violent crime, would increase. By incorporating the 4th and 5th Amendments, by way of the 14th Amendment, so explicitly to the states—and by extension municipal police departments—conservatives and police officers believed that crime would continue climbing, violence would get worse, and cops would not be able, or rather be allowed, to do their job. Such was the fear and the rhetoric, but what we know of the reality suggests something quite different. Although there is some variation, studies tend to suggest that neither *Mapp* nor *Miranda* had any appreciable effect on convictions. Rather, police simply became smarter, some might say more constitutional, at doing their jobs.

The impact of *Mapp* on police effectiveness was mitigated by *Weeks*, which, although applying to the federal government, had an impact on local law enforcement as well. By 1961, when the *Mapp* ruling was handed down, more than half of the states had already incorporated the exclusionary rule into law enforcement practices (Walker, 2011). Still, even considering this, and as Fyfe (1983), Narduilli (1983), and others (e.g., National Study for State Courts, 1986) have found, any effect on convictions from the exclusionary rule for serious crime is negligible. One potential exception to this generalization is with drugs—but even in this case the effect is minimal (Walker, 2011). The reasons why the exclusionary rule "doesn't matter" are several. As Walker (2011) has pointed out, police rarely rely on *physical evidence* to establish probable cause. Consequently, prosecutors rarely rely on physical evidence in their charging decisions. Rather, both parties rely heavily on eyewitness and victim testimony. It is for this reason why we see an exclusionary rule effect (however small) on drug crimes, because such offenses typically *do* rely on the acquisition of physical evidence.

The fact of the matter is that "[o]nce in court, few defendants try to use the exclusionary rule, and even fewer succeed." Additionally, "[j]udges vary greatly in their willingness to invoke the exclusionary rule" (Walker, 2011, p. 113). What's more, just because a defendant is "let off" on a technicality does not guarantee that she will not be convicted after all, if not of the charge pertinent to their motion to suppress evidence, then on another charge. The fear that the exclusionary rule would handcuff the police and keep them from effectively and efficiently doing their job is simply unwarranted. As Walker (2011) concludes, "...critics of the exclusionary rule are guilty of reacting to a few celebrated cases" (p. 113).

Similar conclusions have been reached in terms of *Miranda*'s impact on police work. The opposition started early with Justice White's dissenting opinion, where he quipped: "[this returns] a killer, a rapist or other criminal to the streets and to the environment which produced him, to repeat his crime whenever it pleases him." No credible evidence to date, across fifty years, has supported White's prediction. *Miranda* does not result in cases being thrown out on technicalities for a number of reasons, many of them related to the "problems" with the same dire predictions swarming around the *Mapp* decision. For example, a large number of defendants either waive their *Miranda* rights, or confess prior to the rights being required. Recall that a *Miranda* warning must only be given when a suspect is both in custody and is being interrogated—if only one of those things apply, *Miranda* does not trigger it (although a large percent of police will still Mirandize citizens simply upon arrest). For those suspects who do waive their *Miranda* rights, many still confess once they are confronted with witnesses or physical evidence (Leo, 1996). Consistency among the research has lead Walker (2011) to conclude that "[r]epeal or modification of the *Miranda* warning will not result in more convictions" (p. 117).

Taken together, the concerns surrounding *Mapp* and *Miranda* were unwarranted. *Terry*, however, as has been true throughout this chapter, is a bit of a different beast, both in terms of its social implications (discussed below) and in terms of its impact. If conservatives believed that *Mapp* and *Miranda* handcuffed the police, then liberals believed that *Terry* unleashed the police. Many police departments throughout the United States use the *Terry* decision as their legal rationale for street stops. Most famously, in the 1990s the NYPD, under Chief William Bratton, employed a form of zero-tolerance policing that was aimed at low-level disorder crimes in an effort to net more serious criminals (specifically, gun crimes). Street stops-and-frisks were the most common *modus operandi* of this strategy.

While Bratton and other advocates of zero-tolerance policing maintain that this strategy was successful at removing serious criminals from the street, thereby reducing the New York City crime rate, others are not so convinced (Kelling & Coles, 1998; Zimring, 2008; Rosenfeld, Fornango, & Rengifo, 2007). As Walker (2011) has pointed out, zero-tolerance was not the only thing going on in New York City in the 1990s: there was a national (what is now starting to appear as a near global) reduction in crime rates, a decline in the crack cocaine mark, an astounding increase in law enforcement officers employed by the NYPD, and the introduction of COMPSTAT (to be discussed later in this book). All of which added up to a melange of criminogenic prophylactics that criminal justicians are still working to disentangle (Zimring, 2008). Whatever its empirical reality, the impact of *Terry* on society is of special concern to our topic. It is therefore to the normative impact of the due process revolution that we now turn.

THE NORMATIVE IMPACT OF THE DUE PROCESS REVOLUTION

In spite of the critics' concerns, the exclusionary rule had no substantive impact. As I have suggested throughout this chapter, this lack of meaningful impact on the nature and success of police work did not really matter to the critics. Their problem with the exclusionary rule, and specifically *Mapp* and *Miranda*, was more symbolic than substantive. To law enforcement officers especially, this was nothing short of confirmation of their long-held belief that only the police understood the demands of the work; that they were violently misunderstood by society, including the rest of the criminal justice system; and that their us-versus-them attitude was justified. This would prove explosive at the end of the 1960s.

If police were unhappy with the actions of the Supreme Court in the 1950s and 1960s, along with conservatives in general, liberals were very happy. Their happiness, however, was largely misguided. They, too, thought that rulings like *Mapp* and *Miranda* would have a major impact on the unfair practices of the police. As we have just seen, this was hardly the case. Indeed, there is ample evidence that police largely ignored *Miranda* for the first few years of its existence (Walker, 1998). Liberals' hopes would be vindicated, but only after a decade or so. At that point, "[f]aced with the prospect of losing cases through improper procedures, police departments improved training and supervision...Detectives began conducting more searches with warrants instead of relying on impulsive, warrantless searches...the standard operating procedure...manual became a major tool of police management...[ultimately,] the Court established the principle of accountability" (Walker, 1998, p. 183). In short, policing became more fair and more constitutional (Graham, 1970).

The exclusionary rule, and the press allotted to the Warren Court decisions, also had a "profound, although largely hidden, impact on public attitudes" (Walker, 1998, p. 191). The public were now told, and accepted wholesale, that they could and should *expect* fairness at the hands of the police. Further, if the police treated them with anything *less* than fairness, they had recourse from the courts. As Walker (1998) noted, "Miranda...taught every teenager that he or she had a right to remain silent if arrested." Further, "The heightened awareness of rights brought a lower tolerance for abuse at the hands of the system" (p. 191). This attitude shift would indeed be profound and would prepare the stage for riots *against* the police at the latter end of the 1960s (a topic covered in detail in the next chapter).

At the same time that the public were being told that they "had rights" and did not have to just sit and "take it" when the police "walked over" those rights, police power was expanded in the case of *Terry v. Ohio*. Although legally the jurisprudence behind *Terry*, and its two reasonable suspicion requirements (one for the stop and another for the frisk), may be sound, its ruling went contrary to the Warren Court's trajectory of *limiting* the power of the police to interfere in the lives of people. The force of this contradiction was not lost on the public. As a consequence of the Warren Court, police follow due process most of the time—but one unintended consequence of the

Warren Court's contradictory rulings is that citizens tend to be aware of only a portion of that due process. When police engage in so-called *Terry* stops, citizens may feel that their rights have been violated, when in fact, they have not been (but sometimes they are). This paradox has been a stumbling block for solid police-citizen relationships. Referring again to New York City and its aggressive use of stop-and-frisk, although its effect on crime may still be unclear, its impact on citizen opinion of the police is crystal clear: complaints against the NYPD since the implementation of zero-tolerance have "jumped skyward" (Greene, 1999, p. 171), and the NYPD remains embroiled in federal investigations dealing with whether their stop-and-frisk practices are disproportionately aimed at minorities.

Since the end of the Warren Court, the United States Supreme Court has whittled away at the due process requirements it codified in both *Mapp* and *Miranda*, through a host of exceptions. For example, regarding *Mapp*, the Court has provided for good faith exceptions (e.g., *Massachusetts v. Sheppard*, 1984 and *Arizona v. Evans*, 1995) and the inevitable discovery doctrine (e.g., *Nix v. Williams*, 1984). Regarding *Miranda*, a number of public safety exceptions have been pronounced (e.g., *New York v. Quarles*, 1984), allowances for variation in the verbiage in dictating the *Miranda* rights have been made (e.g., *Duckworth v. Eagan,* 1989), and the Court has indicated that *Miranda* is not necessary during routine DWI stops, including stops that include videotaping the suspect (e.g., *Pennsylvania v. Muniz*, 1990). Almost all of these rulings have been handed down after the Supreme Court took a decidedly conservative bent, starting first with the Rehnquist Court and continuing with the Roberts Court. While *Terry* has seen some clarification from the Court, these rulings have generally not served to curtail the investigative and custodial power of the original 1968 ruling. The developing jurisprudence established (and expanded) in *Terry*, *Mapp*, and *Miranda* continue to be a topic of major importance today, as does their law enforcement application. Indeed, in terms of *Terry*, Walker, Spohn, and DeLone (2012) point out that the use of stop-and-frisk among NYPD officers is still on the increase.

Further, the social ramifications of *Terry* and the virtual paradox it created in the due process revolution cannot be understated. Scholars since Weber (most recently Tom Tyler from Yale) have connected citizen perception of the justice system with their own law abiding behavior. The idea is that folks are more likely to obey the law if they perceive it to be legitimate. Since most folks do not actually *know* the law, their perceptions of its legitimacy are garnered from their interaction with the system. For most Americans (and for most people on American soil, for that matter), their only interaction with the justice system will be through the police. Therefore, a person's willingness to obey the law is directly related to whether they feel that the law treats them fairly—that is, that the *police* treat them fairly. There is no small element of the Thomas Theorem at work here, and the net result places the police in a very awkward and tenuous position. Unfortunately, how the police have historically handled this position has not been conducive to improving their image or their relationship with the public, as will be demonstrated in the following chapter, which considers the race riots of the 1960s.

Chapter Four

Civil Rights and the Police

The Due Process Revolution discussed in the previous chapter was part of a larger paradigmatic shift in American jurisprudence and ethos, one that was moving towards an orientation that was more concerned with social justice. In many ways, this shift culminated in the civil rights movement of the 1950s and 1960s, and would touch essentially all matters of public life and, in many cases, matters of private life. Groundbreaking court cases, such as *Brown v. Board of Education*, negated almost a century of Jim Crow establishment and began breaking down prejudicial norms throughout the country. Such court activism both catalyzed and occurred in tandem with civil rights legislation, most notably the Civil Rights Act of 1964. The police, as a public institution, were not left untouched by the cultural and political changes of the 1950s and 1960s. Unlike so many other institutions, however, the police remained largely unmoved. How could they? The professional model had succeeded too well in isolating and insulating the police from public and political "interference." This, coupled with the historically uneven relationship between the police and minority communities, would explode in five summers of race riots in the 1960s—so many of which were sparked by routine interactions between a police officer and a minority citizen. At the end of these "long hot summers," the professional model would be brought to its knees so dramatically—and violently—that the police would, for the first time in almost fifty years, begin to seriously reconsider both their form and their function under the professional model of Vollmer and, most importantly for the decades under consideration in this book, Vollmer's protege, O. W. Wilson. What the police wanted to do, what the public wanted them to do, and what the government would allow the police to do, all collided toward the end of the 1960s. As Uchida (2005) notes, "[p]olicing in America encountered its most serious crisis in the 1960s." He continues, "The police, in emphasizing its crime fighting ability, had given the public a false expectation they [that is, the police,] had created. As a result, the public image of the police was tarnished" (p. 33).

Just as changes in politics and society were changing in terms of *race*, changes were also occurring in terms of *gender* (and in terms of *religion* and a whole host of social norms, not just in the United States but throughout the Western world). If *law enforcement* is broadly understood in terms of both policing and custody, then women have generally occupied some role in it. That role was always limited, however, to "traditionally" feminine responsibilities, such as jail matronnesses for juveniles, or working with children more generally, or dealing with vice offenders. This all changed in the 1960s and 1970s: In 1971, there were a recorded twelve women police officers, but by 1974, there were almost one thousand women officers—and most of them were patrolling the streets at that point. While American policing remains dominated by men, more women are involved in law enforcement than ever before (although with significant variation throughout the country). Indeed, as of the writing of this chapter, there were over two hundred women chiefs of police in American law enforcement agencies. While this is a fraction of the total number of chiefs (women represent approximately one percent of all chiefs), that number alone is astronomically higher than the total number of women police officers in 1971. In addition, law enforcement enjoys one of the smallest gender gaps when it comes to salary in America. Yet challenges remain, and are, in some senses, holdovers from the challenges experienced by the first patrolling women officers of the 1950s, 1960s, and 1970s. Whether this has changed remains an open-ended question that I will touch on in later chapters. Nevertheless, these concerns were and are felt by millions of American minorities since the 1960s.

This chapter explores these two distinct yet related phenomena. I first consider race riots: their relationship to the police, and the direction to which they forced police to begin moving. I then consider women in policing: their challenges, successes, and what their inclusion meant for policing. In one sense, this chapter considers a series of events that pushed police toward change (that is, the race riots), and an event that represented real movement among police *to* change (that is, the involvement of women in "regular" police work). The race riots represented the old professional model's failures, but the explosion of female (and, for that matter and more generally, minority) officers in agencies throughout America presaged a number of coming changes to American policing. In both cases, these events heralded an expanding role of the American federal government in directing the affairs of local law enforcement agencies. Part of this role would be expressed more indirectly, especially through college education programs funded by the government. Other parts of this role would be more direct and obvious, particularly through the increasing promise of federal monies for carrying out federally designed programs in local law enforcement agencies.

THE LEAD UP TO THE RIOTS

The riots in the 1960s did not occur without warning. In retrospect, they were inevitable. Although their etiology is complex, at least two things presaged the explosion of collective violence in the 1960s *contra* the police: the historically poor relationship between the police and minority communities, and the civil rights movement, itself. The former sowed the seeds of dissent, whereas the latter provided an opportunity for minority communities to reap the unavoidable harvest. Chapter 2 outlined the police-minority community relationship, while chapter 3 discussed some of the events central to the civil rights movement; this section briefly reviews both of these factors. The historical relationship between the police and minority communities is reviewed in terms of its lead up to the race riots, and elements of the civil rights movement that were not mentioned in the preceding chapter are highlighted. As will be demonstrated, many of those aspects central to the professionalism doctrine were also central to the malaise between minorities and the police in America.

Minority Communities and the Police

The relationship between the police and minority communities started out poorly. In the South, one of the first organized police forces was the *slave patrol*: a highly formalized vigilante form of policing explicitly designed to subjugate an entire racial population, African slaves. Policing origins north of what would later be known as the Mason-Dixon line were not all that much better: the creation of the police throughout New England, the Mid-Atlantic, and the Midwest were "encouraged" by sudden waves of European immigration. These immigrants were from "less-than-desirable" European countries that, more often than not, were Catholic in heritage, including Ireland, Italy, and several Eastern European countries, such as Poland. This was not unique to the United States. The Peelian model that American politicians copied from Great Britain was, itself, the result of aristocratic Londoners concerned about the upswell of migrants to the city as a consequence of the Industrial Revolution. As the Crime and Social Justice Association (Institute for the Study of Labor and Economic Crisis, 1982) wrote, "It is clear that the police have *primarily* served to enforce the class, racial, sexual, and cultural oppression that has been an integral part of the development of capitalism in the U.S." (p. 82, emphasis in the original).

Although slavery was abolished in the South in 1863 and throughout the rest of the United States in 1865, the prejudicial heritage of American policing endured throughout the 20th century. In some respects, this was *de jure*. This was especially the case in terms of the administration and enforcement of Black Codes and Jim Crow laws. Even after segregation was declared unconstitutional and Black Codes were removed from state statutes, both empirical and anecdotal evidence continued to evince the prejudicial approach many law enforcement officers used to frame their interactions with minority citizens. Indeed, one of the things that blue ribbon and other government commissions would note in the 60s and 70s was this historic and acrimonious relationship. Although this book is primarily about the 50s, 60s, and 70s, it is important to note that such evidence exists today, as well. For example, one of the most commonly heard cries from both the African American and Latino communities in Los Angeles after the Rodney King tape was made public was a resounding, "finally, LAPD, we caught you on tape!" The riots that ensued after the *not guilty* verdict was handed down in the trial of the four LAPD officers accused of beating King illegally were, in fact, begun with regular invocations of the 1960s (cf. the VH1 documentary *Uprising: Hip Hop and the LA Riots*).

This historically unhealthy relationship was aggravated by the professional model of policing. In creating this model, Vollmer borrowed heavily from the "ideal" bureaucracy as articulated by Weber. This meant, among other things, that policing, as an organization, operated as what institutional theorists would call a *closed model*. A closed model organization is characterized by a lack of input from the environment. Rather, the organization is more task-oriented, focused on the *how to* versus the *what happens*. This task-oriented behavior takes place under an assumption that tasks are routine and take place in a stable environment. This assumption is not true: social environments are in constant flux. Because closed models—such as the police—are based on this faulty assumption, and because they do not consider input from that fluid environment, a situation arises where the environment moves on, but the organisation does not. What's worse, the organization may not even be aware that the environment in which it works has moved on. This scenario aptly describes the situation the police found themselves in at the start of the 1960s: the professional model had made sure that they were stuck in pre-civil rights movement practices, *and* were unable to understand that the civil rights movement would *demand* that their behavior toward minority communities change. This social disconnect would explode in riots against the police toward the denouement of the civil rights movement. It is to that civil rights movement that we now turn.

The Civil Rights Movement

The civil rights movement, in terms of the race riots against the police, can be understood in terms of two things. First, it legalized and justified the sense of anger among minorities against not only the police, but against the political and economic establishment of the United States, generally. Second, it endowed minority communities with tools to combat against centuries of legal and *de facto* oppression. Together, these two factors served to bring to light the unjustness of police behavior vis-a-vis minorities to politicians who were willing to do something about it, and also served to legitimize the suffering of minorities at the hands of the police. Its effect was therefore both legal and normative: it was no longer reasonable, moral, or allowable to use the police to oppress an entire population.

Central to the civil rights movement was the economic condition of minorities and minority communities. The economic status of African American communities in the United States has never been comparable to their white counterparts. Throughout the 1950s and 1960s (and into contemporary American society), African American neighborhoods were characterized by low levels of education, in tandem with high levels of school dropouts, a non-trivially high number of single-parent families, and exceptionally high levels of drug and alcohol abuse, and criminal activity and fear of crime (Williams & Murphy, 1990). This characterization was hardly novel, so what pushed African American communities to respond with riots? First, there was the civil rights movement itself which encouraged African American communities and leaders to push for improved conditions at the societal and political levels. Riots were a part of this response (Walker, 1998).

In addition to this, there were elements of American policing that helped light the fuse that resulted in the explosion of riots throughout the 1960s. First, the very nature of American policing under the professional model retarded efforts to fully integrate African American officers. Recall that the hallmark of the professional policing model was *bureaucracy*. One of the hallmarks of bureaucracies is conservativism. That is, a bureaucracy is, by design, not meant to change. Or, if it does change, to do so deliberately and slowly. Additionally, bureaucratic organizations are not designed to take input from the environment. What these two characteristics mean for the police is that while the rest of the United States government and society were being caught in the rush of the civil rights movement, the police were effectively left behind. They simply could not keep up, because they were not meant to. But a public agency that does not listen and adjust to the changing social climate risks losing legitimacy—and this is exactly what happened to the police during the 1960s (Walker, 1977). Related to the closed-model nature of the professional policing model was the very reason this particular model came into existence. Remember that the professionalism movement in general—and in particular for the police—began largely in reaction to widespread *political influence*. In other words, the professionalism movement began to keep politics *out* of policing. The civil rights movement was many things, including *political*—and as such, professional policing was well equipped to keep its reach away from policing (Walker, 1977). The riots were a direct, public, and violent response to the institutional apathy of the police to social changes.

Second, policing in the United States at the latter half of the professional era was impersonal (again, an inheritance from the Weberian bureaucratic model), aggressive, and characterized by an *us versus them* attitude that pit the police against everybody who was not a cop. As we saw in previous chapters, the police felt as if the entire nation despised and distrusted them—despite the fact that it was the police who were (at least, according to themselves) protecting those very critics. This was only exacerbated by both politicians and the United States Supreme Court, to say nothing of the media. Everyone seemed to dislike the police. This ethos pushed the police into a deeper isolation from the very communities which they served, including the minority community. Such a breakdown in communication would also contribute to riots against the police. This lack of communication often became explosive when police engaged in more, and more aggressive, patrol. Indeed, it was often such aggressive patrolling, which was itself often perceived by citizens as being unfair, that sparked so many of the race riots against the police in the 1960s (Walker, 1977).

As Walker (1977) points out in his book, *A Critical History of Police Reform*, race riots were nothing new to the American landscape—including those directed against the police. For example, there were numerous race riots against the police during the early 1900s, and especially devastating riots during 1943 in Detroit, New York City, and Los Angeles. What was so different in the 1960s, perhaps, is that at this point, the Civil Rights Movement had gained significant momentum. As Williams and Murphy (1990) argue, the police were seen as the symbol of everything wrong with American government and society as it applied to minority communities. Given the role of the police as formal agents of social control, and given that, as we have already seen, the police were historically deployed to maintain the *status quo* contra the interests of those minority communities, this should come as no surprise. Therefore, when minority communities' demand for change took the form of race riots, it is no less surprising that they would target the police.

THE RACE RIOTS OF THE 1960S

Not only were race riots nothing new to American political history, so too were the explanations and recommendations following each of these race riots hardly novel. By the time the race riots of the 1960s came around, commentators and pundits of racial and class affairs in the United States were already predicting—and rightfully bemoaning—the inevitable response by the government (Walker, 1998). The actual response would, indeed, be different this go-around. In part, this was due to the events described in the preceding section, most notably the civil rights movement. In addition, the catalyst of the riots of the 1960s (and, for that matter, the 1950s), were different than those of earlier generations. While race riots during the first half of the 20th century were largely the result of racial tensions between *communities*, the "new form of riot usually began with a confrontation between blacks and the police over a relatively trivial matter" (Johnson, 1981, p. 132). This new focus on the police at the riot level would result in a police-centered response on the part of the federal government. Indeed, the recommendations made by the federal government were in response not just to the rioters, but more especially to the police and their activities before, during, and after the riots.

The race riots of the 1960s have been called "The Long Hot Summers," as it was during the summer time that riots were happening across the United States. The Long Hot Summers lasted from 1964 to 1968, and occurred in major cities throughout the United States. The very first riot started Harlem, New York City, on July 16, 1964. It was sparked when an off-duty white police officer, Thomas Gilligan, shot and killed a fifteen-year-old African American teenage boy, James Powell. Gilligan was shopping when he saw a potential confrontation developing between Powell, his friends, and a white superintendent who was trying to chase several African American youth from his property by using a hose. After firing a warning shot, Gilligan shot and killed Powell. This incident was witnessed by several dozen bystanders, most of whom were African American. The Black community then responded with riots against the New York Police Department that lasted two full days, and resulted in one fatality and almost twenty citizen injuries and twelve police officer injuries. The effects of the Harlem riots of 1964 were not limited to the NYPD, however—they spread throughout the United States in a series of riots that summer, including in Philadelphia, Rochester, and Jersey City (Walker, 1998).

Over the next four years, race riots against the police would continue throughout the country. The year following the Harlem riots saw one of the most destructive riots in American 20th century history, in the Watts area of Los Angeles. This riot lasted for six days, and resulted in thousands of injuries and approximately four thousand arrests. The property destruction escalated to over $40 million. Most disconcertedly were the thirty-four fatalities (Walker, 1998). This pattern would persist for the following three years. In 1966, there were serious race riots in Chicago, Cleveland, Omaha, Dayton, San Francisco, and Atlanta—among thirty-eight other major American cities. And in 1967, a riot in Newark lasted for five days and left twenty-three dead. The culminating race riot occurred in Detroit that same year, which, after a week, resulted in forty-three deaths and over $40 million worth in damages.

It was this latter riot that ultimately led to the federal government's undivided attention to several years of consistent summer race riots. Their response took the form of commission reports—most particularly the report published as *The Challenge of Crime in a Free Society*, and the Kerner commission's publication, *Report of the National Advisory Commission on Civil Disorders*.

The Challenge of Crime in a Free Society

The President's Commission on Law Enforcement and Administration of Justice's publication, *The Challenge of Crime in a Free Society*, appeared two years after the commission was constituted under President Lyndon Johnson in 1965. Both the title of the commission and of its culminating publication are telling. This commission was concerned not so much with *crime* as it was with society's response to crime in the form of the criminal justice *system*. That term, *system*, was first put to good use to describe the institutions that are American criminal justice in that report, and it has stuck ever since, despite several attempts to do away with it (e.g., Kraska's attempt with his 2003 publication to relabel the criminal justice system as the American crime control apparatus). No other such nomenclatures have caught on, however. This must be due, at least in part, to the revolutionary notion of understanding the component parts of American criminal justice *as a system*—as a coherent ecology where each part impacts both the nature and behavior of the other parts. Prior to the 1960s, the notion that the American courts, prisons, jails, probation departments, and law enforcement agencies were part of a systematic whole was not held by either academics or professionals. Rather, each part was understood as being just one other public service. The *systems theory* of organization, popular in institutional psychology at the time, heavily influenced this new conceptualization of what American criminal justice meant and did (Klofas, Hipple, & McGarrell, 2010; this change in American public organization is discussed in depth in chapter 6).

In a similar vein, the title suggested the tension between *rights* and *order* so prevalent in much of American history. As it indicates, *crime* poses a challenge in a free society. It does so on a number of levels. First, crime threatens freedom. Indeed, one way to understand *crime* in a free society is the unlawful limiting of another's liberty. What is larceny, after all, but limiting someone's liberty to possess property? Homicide is, of course, the ultimate expression of precluding the free exercise of one's liberty. But the title, *The Challenge of Crime in a Free Society*, presupposes another tension between *rights* and *orders*, specifically, and again by definition, *laws* inherently *limit* freedom. Jeremy Bentham famously stated that "every law is an infraction of liberty". Just as the burglar infringes on the liberty to own property, so, too, do taxes limit the freedom of owning property. And, again, a police officer lawfully taking a dangerous suspect's life—or a doctor administering the lethal drugs during a state execution—forever limit the free agency of the deceased individual. Or, less dramatically and certainly more commonly, a highway patrol officer pulling a driver over for speeding is limiting that driver's freedom to drive as quickly as he pleases. All laws—both in the literal sense of codified norms and in the abstract Blackian sense of the behavior or the administration of law (Black, 1979)—*require* that someone's liberty be infringed. In a democracy, this creates an usual paradox that plays out regularly on the streets between the police and civilians—sometimes with violent repercussions. In a very real way, the President's Commission's *The Challenge of Crime in a Free Society* was the government's first attempt to understand the etiology of the race riots—and tellingly, they looked at the behavior of law through the administration of justice, rather than the behavior of individuals.

The Challenge of Crime in a Free Society painted a bleak picture of urban America, both in terms of crime and the environment. The report reflected the evolving and prevailing political and academic opinions of the time regarding the etiology of crime—namely, that its source was to be found in the individual's surroundings rather than in the individual himself. As the report noted early on: "One hypothesis about everyday crime in the slums is that much of it is a blind reaction to the conditions of slum living" (p. 37). Additionally, the report noted that poor parenting, a lack of qualified social institutions, and an anomic gap between goals and means contributed to criminal behavior. All of these were deemed *social* problems, and therefore outside not only the purview but the very control of the police. Yet as the report also noted, it was *to* the police that many disadvantaged communities looked for solving the rising crime problem—including the race riots. This expectation, as I have noted elsewhere, was partly a product of the police professionalism movement. This problem was exacerbated by the poor relationship between inner city neighborhoods—which were largely *minority* neighborhoods—and the police. *The Challenge of Crime in a Free Society* noted the sad irony that, although inner city "slums" needed the police the most, they are populated by individuals who distrust the police and who were unwilling to help them in any capacity beyond reporting a crime via an anonymous phone call—and even that was not a guarantee.

In answering the question, *why do citizens in disadvantaged communities distrust the police so much*, the President's Commission offered several answers. In direct regard to the race riots, they stated that "the principal objects of attack were most often just those people or institutions, insofar as they were within reach, that the rioters thought of as being their principal oppressors..." (p. 37). The Commission submitted that this involved *all* white-owned and controlled establishments, including and especially "policemen"

(p. 37). The Commission also pointed the finger of blame at the police in terms of how they treated, or rather mistreated, minorities: "[Protesters] stated quite explicitly they had been protesting against, indeed trying to call the attention of the white community to, police misconduct" (p. 38). The problem was not always one of officer misconduct, at least not in the technical sense:

> Commission studies also showed, and in this finding responsible police officers concur, that too many policemen do misunderstand and are indifferent to minority-group aspirations, attitudes, and customs, and that incidents involving physical or verbal mistreatment of minority-group citizens do occur and do contribute to the resentment against police that some minority-group members feel." (p. 100)

In that single sentence the Commission singled out the police as part of the cause—and the Report would insist that they were a major cause—of the race riots. Police were ignorant of the minority community and apathetic toward this ignorance. And under a professional model of policing this is how law enforcement was set up to operate. But doing so created a horrible public relations problem in the most literal sense of the expression *public relations*. The Commission sardonically opined that "this is the problem that is usually—and politely—referred to as 'police-community relations.' It is overwhelmingly a problem of the relations between the police and the minority-group community" (p. 99). But just as the police at the end of the 19th century and the beginning of the 20th century underwent a paradigmatic shift from a despotic system of patronage to a bureaucratic system based on the Social Progressive movement, so, too, would the police need to catch up to the now open-systems model that was sweeping American polity. Under an open-systems model, and in contrast to the closed-system model of a Weberian bureaucracy, an organization does adapt to its institutional and social environment.

The recommendations of the President's Commission in *The Challenge of Crime in a Free Society* reflected this position. They noted that there needed to be change not only in the criminal justice system, but also how involved citizens were with that system. To have any impact on crime, the Report insisted that the public and the newly-christened Criminal Justice System needed to work together. But just as they indicated that the impetus of the problem relations between the police and minority community was largely the fault of the police, so, too, did they note that the Criminal Justice System—that is, the police—needed to take the first steps toward change. This was only the paradigm that the President's Commission recommended the police undergo—it inhered a number of philosophical, strategic, and tactical recommendations. Many of these recommendations would lead to other events surrounding the 60s and 70s that are the focus of this book. But *The*

Challenge of Crime in a Free Society was not the only commission report about the police that came out of the 1960s. To this end, I now turn to the Kerner Commission's 1968 *Report of the National Advisory Commission on Civil Disorders.*

Report of the National Advisory Commission on Civil Disorders

The Kerner Commission (named after the Illinois governor who chaired it, Otto Kerner) was established by President Lyndon Johnson in direct response to the growing racial unrest as witnessed by the riots. As the report itself indicates, President Johnson tasked the commission with answering three questions: "What happened? Why did it happen? [And w]hat can be done to prevent it from happening again?" (p. 1). After several months of investigation, the Commission's answer came by way of an almost six-hundred page document (in its Bantam Books' edition, copyright 1968; the demand for the book was so high among the American public that it went through over ten printings in that first year alone), the *Report of the National Advisory Commission on Civil Disorders*, also known simply as the *Kerner Report*. Similar to *The Challenge of Crime in a Free Society*, the *Kerner Report* answers these questions with an appeal to social conditions. The Kerner Commission did not hold anything back: Among the social conditions it cited was American white racism. The Commission famously quipped on the starting page that "This is our basic conclusion: Our nation is moving toward two societies, one black, one white—separate and unequal" (p. 1).

The etiology of this inequality was multivariate, and included, *inter alia*, widespread discrimination and segregation, with fatal ramifications for the black population in terms of both employment and education; a series of black migrations (especially from the South to the North) to cities, in tandem with white exoduses from cities to suburbs; and the subsequent creation of inner city black ghettos. All of these factors only added to the anomic feeling described in the black community already noted in *The Challenge of Crime in a Free Society*. They also led to violence in the black, urban ghettos, mass poverty, and increased resentment against white society. Such feelings of powerless and racial resentment, the Kerner Report noted, facilitated the Black Power movement, which was nurtured on both racial pride and alienation. The Commission concluded that, while these causes were important—even vital—for explaining and preventing the riots, the immediate cause was the police and their treatment of black citizens: "All the major outbursts of recent years...were precipitated by routine arrests of Negroes for minor offenses by white police" (p. 206). Police practices were the catalyst that more often than not "sparked" the race riots preceding (and following) the Commission's investigation.

Importantly, the Commission noted in their report that it was not, however, quite that simple. For example, "the causes of recent racial disorders are imbedded in a massive tangle of issues and circumstances—social, economic, political, and psychological—which arise out of the historical pattern of Negro-white relations in America. These factors are both complex and interacting...and the consequences of one disorder, generating new grievances and new demands, become the causes of the next" (p. 203). As far as the police were concerned, "It is the convergence of all these factors that makes the role of the police so difficult and so significant" (p. 206). The Report continued:

> But the police are not merely the spark. In discharge of their obligation to maintain order and insure public safety in the disruptive conditions of ghetto life, they are inevitably involved in sharper and more frequent conflicts with ghetto residents than with the residents of other areas. Thus, to many Negroes police have come to symbolize white power, white racism and white repression. And the fact is that many police do reflect and express these white attitudes. The atmosphere of hostility and cynicism is reinforced by a widespread perception among Negroes of the existence of police brutality and corruption, and of a "double standard" of justice and protection—one for Negroes and one for whites. (p. 206)

So although police were *at fault* in starting the riots, they could only be *part* of the solution. But the key to the Report, as far as this book is concerned, is that the federal government was, indeed, squarely faulting the American police in causing dangerous riots—something which flies in the face of their constitutional mandate to *maintain order*.

The very police response to the riots was itself exceptionally counterproductive: It was swift, brutal, and violent (Williams & Murphy, 1990). The Commission recognized that whether the police were the ultimate, penultimate, or distal cause of the riots was somewhat—at least in the immediate—moot: police response to the riots and to minority communities in general needed to change. In a reflection of several of the recommendations put forward by the President's Commission in *The Challenge of Crime in a Free Society*, the Kerner Commission recommended several changes in police-citizen relations that would later evolve into what we now refer to as community oriented policing. For example, they encouraged the development and improvement of "community service functions"—that is, non-law enforcement activities: "The Commission believes that police cannot, and should not, resist becoming involved in community service matters. There will be benefits for law enforcement no less than for public order" (p. 318). Along with this, the Commission recommended a number of community relations programs designed to both train police in public relations and to draw communities and the police together.

The Commission similarly recommended that police agencies hire more minority officers, promote minority officers to influential supervisory and administrative positions, and provide minority officers more equal opportunities to engage in police work. It was common prior to the 1960s for black police officers only to be allowed to patrol majority black neighborhoods (see chapter 2 for an overview). Now the Commission was recommending that this discriminatory practice be dropped. The expectation was that black officers would relate better to majority black neighborhoods, and that they would influence their white counterparts to do so, as well. Police departments did make these changes, but the benefits were not immediately forthcoming: Minority officers were often in a double bind where they were treated disrespectfully by minority communities (especially young black men), and treated poorly by their white counterparts. The belief among many white officers was that black policemen would treat minorities more leniently than they deserved. The consequence of this double marginality was that black officers initially treated minority citizens *more* harshly than white officers, both in response to the disrespect shown them by young black men, and to alleviate the concerns of their white colleagues by showing without equivocation that they would not be more lenient toward minorities. Eventually, as American police forces became more diverse and representative of the populations whom they served, this double marginality would decline significantly (Walker, Spohn, DeLone, 2012).

One of the most important series of recommendations made by the Kerner Commission was to streamline and enforce the complaint process. Indeed, a number of their recommendations, either directly or indirectly, concerned citizen complaints against the police. In some cases, this meant better screening of officer candidates, while in others it meant keeping "problem" officers away from minority communities. Mostly, though, these recommendations suggested that citizen complains be easier to make, investigated with more thoroughness and seriousness, and have meaningful sanctions attached to them. The Commission laid out several of these recommendations thusly (cf. page 311):

> Making a complaint should be easy. It should be possible to file a grievance without excessive formality... A specialized agency, with adequate funds and staff, should be created separate from other municipal agencies, to handle, investigate and to make recommendations on citizen complaints...The complaining party should be able to participate in the investigation and in any hearings, with right representation by counsel...The results of the investigation should be made public.

As Walker (2005) would point out some fifty years later in his book *The New World of Police Accountability*, these changes were slow in coming—at times did not come at all, or if they did, came with several strings and amendations attached. This is due in some part to the fact that commissions, such as both the Kerner and President's Commissions discussed here, "lack any capacity to implement their own recommendations and ensure that reform occurs" (p. 36). Additionally, the bureaucratic nature of police precludes—at least hinders—any progress that includes "external input," such as complaints. Nevertheless, as will be seen in chapter 9, the recommendations and the very existence of the *Kerner Report* would have lasting impacts on police behavior and form in the United States. And the same should be said for *The Challenge of Crime in a Free Society*. One such impact would be through the creation of LEAP—the Law Enforcement Education Program. The effect of this federal program has been so lasting it is worth digressing somewhat to discuss it and its ramifications.

The Law Enforcement Education Program

Clearly, the race riots caught the attention of the federal government. In response, the Office of Law Enforcement Assistance was liquidated and reborn as the Law Enforcement Assistance Administration (LEAA) under the Omnibus Crime Control and Safe Streets Act of 1968 (Uchida, 2005; it, too, would be dissolved in the 1980s and would eventually evolve into the Office of Justice Programs). Pursuant to the recommendations of the President's and Kerner Commissions, the LEAA issued a number of grants aimed at understanding the social causes of crime. Such grants drew the attention of university sociologists, and helped to create a new discipline (or subdiscipline) of criminological research: criminal justice. Although these two terms—criminology and criminal justice—are often confounded in contemporary academe, there was and remains a distinction between the two. Whereas the former is the study of the etiology of criminal behavior and crime rates, the latter is the study of the social response to crime and deviance. College criminal justice programs were founded based on the realization—brought about by the riots and the subsequent commission reports on the riots—that policing involved more "peacekeeping" than "crime fighting," despite the fact that everyone tended to focus on the second aspect of police work, to the detriment of the first aspect. "Everyone" included those who trained police cadets in academies. The idea that if police would focus more on keeping the peace through community service then relations between the police and minority communities would improve took hold across the United States, and was reinforced and facilitated through a number of college criminal justice programs.

These criminal justice programs were in nature part-academic, part-technical. Students were taught social theory, but especially were taught *how* to be police. They were often run and taught by current or retired law enforcement professionals. (This "cop-shop" approach to criminal justice would begin to disappear starting in the 1990s, as criminal justice departments began hiring only doctorate holding professors, without regard to any previous professional experience.) To be sure, college level criminal justice programs were not new—arguably, the program developed by August Vollmer at Berkeley fits this mold, and many "criminology" programs prior to the 1970s could better be described as criminal justice in nature and application. The difference in the late 1960s and 1970s was in regard to the attention such programs received from the federal government. There was a proliferation of criminal justice programs in college campuses across the United States throughout the 1970s exactly because of the LEAA, which funded such programs and students through their new Law Enforcement Education Program (LEEP). As the Office of Justice Programs noted in their 1996 publication *LEAA/OJP Retrospective: 30 Years of Federal Support to State and Local Criminal Justice*, LEEP was responsible for over "100,000 students to attend more than 1,000 colleges and universities. A significant majority of current criminal justice leaders around the country are LEEP alumni" (p. 3).

The LEAA, LEEP, and the multitude of criminal justice programs and students that they funded would greatly impact the police by drawing issues of crime and justice to a broader audience of academics (Uchida, 2005). Throughout the 1970s, such academics would use the scientific method to call traditional, that is, professional model police practices into question. Although this research would take awhile to effect change in American law enforcement, it would greatly affect such change. Additionally, it would lead to a number of policing strategies, with greater or lesser success, such as community oriented policing, problem oriented policing, intelligence based policing, and evidenced based policing. A number of theoretical approaches would also inform police practices, such as Routine Activities Theory (Cohen & Felson, 1979) and its practical counterpart, Situational Crime Prevention (Clarke, 1983). Perhaps the most important consequence of LEAA and LEEP would be New York City Police Department's COMPSTAT and its extensive adoption among other American law enforcement agencies. However one conceptualizes it, modern American policing has shifted from an *ad hoc* patrol paradigm to one aligned more closely with the scientific model. These changes are due in large part to the programs, studies, and students funded by the LEAA via LEEP. The subsequent research would challenge police practices in a way that could not be ignored—empirically. Understanding this research and its consequences for the American policing ethos is so important that chapter seven is devoted to its exploration.

The race riots were part of a larger social movement in the United States that politically manifested as the Civil Rights Movement. This movement included not only aspects of *race* but aspects of *gender*. Just as the police were not "immune" to the social and political changes relative to race during this time period, neither were they "safe" from issues surrounding gender equality. Women police officers were given more opportunities than ever before during the 1960s and especially the 1970s (many of these changes were made because of funding requirements from LEAA). Although American police agencies are more representative now than ever before in terms of *race*, the profession remains overwhelmingly *male* in make-up. Nevertheless, it is also one of the occupations where the gender gap in pay is relatively small, thanks to changes in the role of women police officers that occurred during the 1970s.

THE CHANGING ROLE OF WOMEN IN POLICING

Like so many of the subjects covered in this book, the topic of women in policing deserves a much lengthier treatment, such as that offered by Allan Duffin's (2010) *History in Blue: 160 Years of Women Police, Sheriffs, Detectives, and State Troopers.* Although there were changes to the role of women in policing in the 50s and 60s, it was in the 1970s where the most dramatic changes were seen. Prior to the 1970s, women barely made up two percent of the American police force: in 1971 there were twelve women *patrol* officers across the entire United States, but already by 1974 this number increased to about one thousand. The assignments that were given to women also changed in the 1970s. In the 1950s and 1960s, those women who were police officers were given stereotypically female roles, such as working with female prisoners or juveniles, rather than being allowed to patrol. By the mid-1970s, women were regularly being assigned to patrol (Duffin, 2010).

There are several reasons why the number and roles of women police officers changed in the 1970's and not earlier. The largest stumbling block was the patriarchal nature of industrial America and the androcentric character of policing. The police—and to some extent the public—did not believe that policing was an appropriate job for women, nor that women were capable of doing the work. There were concerns that women were too "emotional" for the work, and not physically strong enough for the requirements of the job. Vollmer's protege, O. W. Wilson (1963), a powerful police reformer in his own right, wrote in his seminal police text, *Police Administration*, that women should not be in leadership positions, even those over traditionally female domains. For example:

> As a general rule the head of the youth division should be a man with a well-rounded police experience rather than a woman, because (1) men have a better understanding of the attitudes of other divisions and especially of the detective division toward crime-prevention work, (2) men are better able to win cooperative support from other members of the department, (3) men are physically and emotionally able to withstand the pressure of the work and are, therefore,

less likely to become irritable and overcritical under emotional stress, and (4) men are usually better supervisors of women than are other women. (p. 334)

Taken-for-granted "wisdom" such as this lead to prejudice among male officers who didn't want to work with women. These less tangible stumbling blocks created very tangible challenges for women wanting to be police officers as agencies rushed to create hiring requirements that would *de facto*, if not *de jure*, preclude women's entry into policing. Such measures included height and weight requirements, and the need for women to hold a college degree (Duffin, 2010). Within time, these requirements would be eliminated—but not without the active efforts of women and legislators.

Although women and men police officers enjoy a closer parity in their salaries today, this was obviously not the case in the 1960s. Women officers therefore hit the courts as their first line of offense, focusing on equal pay, and also on ending sexual harassment by their male colleagues, and winning cases all along the way. Throughout the 60s and into the 70s, a number of bills would be passed to further reduce discrimination against women in policing (as well as other public sector jobs), including the 1963 Equal Pay Act, the establishment of the 1964 Equal Employment Opportunity Commission, and the 1972 Equal Employment Opportunity Act. This final piece of legislation had, among other things, two major impacts: it applied the hiring and salary requirements of the 1964 act to local political bodies, instead of only to the federal government as it was originally written, and it facilitated closer scrutiny of police agencies for discrimination (Duffin, 2010).

As far as women were concerned, then, the 1970s can be seen as a time of great flux in terms of policing. Not only were there more women police officers, but more women police were doing "real" policing. To be sure, challenges continued from the policing profession—a profession that largely remains male dominated. As Duffin (2010) points out, women continued to face sexual harassment, harsher sanctions when involved in disciplinary proceedings, and were often treated as being less "courageous" than their male counterparts, especially whenever they "allowed" their male supervisors to call the shots. Walker, Spohn, and Delone (2012) describe the situation of female police officers during this time as a "double bind." Because of the masculine nature of the police force, female officers had a choice: either give up their role as police officer and maintain their femininity, and thus be relegated to the stereotypically feminine work of victims services, vice, and juveniles, or give up their femininity and get to do "real" police work. The price of the latter "choice" was being labeled a "dyke" at a time when homosexuality was still illegal in most states (Martin, 1979).

It is an irony—both for the writers of *The Challenge of Crime in a Free Society* and the *Kerner Report* and for those policemen opposing the integration of policewomen—that most research has borne out that female police officers behave in ways strikingly similar to their male counterparts. Given that both men and women now receive the same training, this is no surprise. This is *now*, however—initially their training was sometimes different from male cadets (Duffin, 2010). It is also true that, although no police agency in America that I am aware of even approaches male-female representativeness (large city agencies, which, by and large, are more representative than small city agencies, are, on average, around 12 percent female—see any year of the FBI's *Uniform Crime Reports* for details), agencies are more representative now than they were then, and the double bind characteristic of female policing has diminished considerably (Walker, Spohn, Delone, 2012). We are getting ahead of ourselves somewhat, but the improved situation of police women in the United States today is because of how police agencies had to adapt to the changing social and legal landscape of the 1960s and 1970s. As Duffin (2010) points out, women still face both harassment and discrimination in the police force, but the situation has improved considerably. Just as one example, it is more common now than ever for women to hold supervisory and administrative positions, including several police chiefs of major American cities (e.g., Cathy Lanier of the Washington, D.C. Metropolitan Police). The current status of women in policing is an enduring example that policing would *have* to change—there was no other choice.

CONCLUSIONS

Although perhaps oversimplifying the situation, it is no less accurate to admit that the race riots occurred because of police mistreatment of minority communities. And it is certainly accurate to submit that rioting would, in turn, dramatically change the form and function of the police. While some of these changes were more immediate, most were long in coming, as will be laid out in more detail in chapter 9. It cannot be the police, therefore, that were responsible for the riots' cessation, at least not in great part. As Johnson (1981) has pointed out, why the riots ended after 1968 remains an open-ended question. Such open-ended questions are more common in criminological research than one might find comfortable. For example, partisan opinion to the contrary, why the crime rate fell across the United States (and most certainly across most of the Western and industrial world) during the 1990s remains a mystery (Zimring, 2008). Part of the mystery has less to do with the etiology of these phenomena and more to do with the current state of criminological epistemology, which can accurately be described as exceedingly reductionist and univariate. The end result of such positivistic myopia is a hodge-podge of theoretical statements all predicting the same thing with the same variables in different ways, but with an uber-focus on *their* pet variable (e.g., the low self-control of Gottfredson and Hirschi's [1990] General Theory of Crime). Again, as Zimring (2008) concluded in *The Great American Crime Decline*, the causes of the American crime drop cannot be successfully understood with an appeal to any single variable; so, too, with the end of the riots. As Johnson (1981) has suggested, this may have been due to new social programs, a diminution of violence as a political tool, and yes, even better policing practices. Most likely, it was a combination of these factors in interaction, among others that, for the time being, are buried in the sociologist's black box of "measurement error."

One of the less often recognized agents of change at this time period were police unions. As the federal government was calling for oversight of police agencies, unions were fighting to ensure that such oversight was fair. Unions were responsible for both disciplinary due process and collective bargaining agreements—often using the same arguments politicians and activists used to pass civil rights legislation during the 1960s. Unions therefore demonstrated how police departments could change and adapt while maintaining their identity and professional purposes of crime fighting. In this way, the police unions set the stage for greater integration of both minority—especially black—officers and women officers (Walker, 1998). In some instances, the changes were mere veneers—what the Crime and Social Justice Association (Institute for the Study of Labor and Economic Crisis, 1982) referred to as the "iron fist and the velvet glove," a clever analogy that meant police were *doing* the same things while giving the *appearance* of doing otherwise. As time would pass, police would be less and less able to keep up appearances of this nature. Although there remain challenges for both minority and women officers, things are better. One can say the same for minority communities: although things could be better, they are certainly better than they were fifty years ago. Despite the closed, bureaucratic policing model of August Vollmer and the professionalism movement, *change* did happen, and would continue to move forward among police agencies around the nation. The federal commissions, unions, and the successes of the women's employment rights movement radically put the professional model into question in such a way that police administrators could not ignore (Uchida, 2005).

Theoretically, the effect of the race riots and women's movement was to call into question the legitimacy of the police as an institution. As briefly discussed in chapter 2, the professional model of police-*cum*-crime fighters was seriously flawed insofar as police, under this model, were incapable of effecting a reduction in crime. Their legitimacy—that is, their "right to exist"—as an institution had to be sought elsewhere, therefore. For the police, legitimacy was to be found in a heavy investment in PR. This investment would pay off with substantial dividends: politicians and enfranchised Americans would be convinced that the police were the only thing keeping them from chaos and disorder. It would take the violent riots of the 1960s, against which the police were impotent *and* responsible, and the successful integration of women police officers *contra* stereotyped police images of the necessary masculinity of the job, to shatter this image and hence the legitimacy of the police. As a consequence, the very existence of policing as an institution was in jeopardy. Change was not only inevitable, it was essential.

The most sweeping change that would roll out of these social movements was a change in how policing would be approached. The traditional cold, calculated framework of professional policing, epitomized by Joe Friday's "Just the facts, ma'am," would eventually give way to a framework that was more collaborative and problem-solving in nature. The systems theory that became popular in the 1960s is at least in part responsible for this change. Police agencies would recognize that they had two constituents with whom they needed to work more closely: the public and the rest of the newly-minted "criminal justice system". Seeing itself as part of a larger crime control picture would in due course diminish the isolated nature of policing and break down the walls of its closed bureaucratic model. But the transformation from closed- to open-model would be hindered and ultimately incomplete because of other important ideological and organizational characteristics of policing against which such a wide-sweeping organizational change must combat: the conservative nature of police and policing.

Chapter Five

A Due Process Approach in the Face of Police Conservatism

The civil rights movement, especially as manifested in the race riots of the 1960s, was just one example of society moving in one direction and the police staying firmly planted in a professional and conservative ethos. The two go hand in hand: as pointed out in previous chapters, police are themselves conservative in nature, and the police as an institution is a bureaucracy which is, again, by nature, designed to conserve. That is, police agencies were designed to resist change, and to work as though they existed in an environmental vacuum. Not only was change not forthcoming among police agencies in response to the demands of the public and politicians, but the social distance between police and public was about to get wider. And this gap encompassed not only society, but other criminal justice agencies as well. The irony—discussed in more detail in the next chapter—that criminal justice agencies were now being conceptualized as one coherent whole *system*, while simultaneously the police were not keeping up with the changes in those other agencies, should be clear. The gap would be fortified by the various approaches to crime that the police would continue to take compared to the more progressive approaches that the justice system would adopt during the 1950s and 1960s.

To understand these different approaches, I borrow from Herbert Packer's (1964) well known dual taxonomy model that distinguishes between crime control and due process. While other criminal justice agencies—and the public—had embraced a model that could be described as due process, police staunchly maintained a crime control approach. In addition, while police and police agencies were punitive by nature, the response to crime *du jour* could best be described as treatment oriented. Although punishment can be part of a progressive criminal justice agenda (e.g., see Howard Zehr's 2002 book,

The Little Book of Restorative Justice), such was not the case in the 1950s and 1960s—neither among the police nor the rest of the criminal justice system. The fact is that most students of criminal justice misapply his two models, assuming that they are accurate ways of describing how the system does work. Rather, Packer's models describe how people believe the system *should* work. The crime control and due process models are therefore commentary on the perceptions held by people about the criminal justice system. As the Thomas Theorem teaches us, however, perceptions can be just as potent as reality when the two are confounded. This was the case in the 1950s and 1960s: perceiving a change in the wind of which they had no desire to be a part, police retreated into a conservative ethos and isolated themselves from the *body politic* that they served.

As we have already explored, however, the police could not maintain this social isolation. Doing so would risk their legitimacy and therefore their existence. Further, the federal government was not going to let them sulk in their conservatism. As we saw in the last chapter, the race riots opened the door for the federal government to have unprecedented say in what the police should and should not do. And now that the police were conceptualized as merely part of a criminal justice system, rather than the thin blue line between chaos and peace, the deliberateness to remain apart from social and political winds would be attenuated. Being part of this system would come with an enormous psychic cost on police, adding to their feeling that the world was against them. Ultimately, the phenomena covered in this chapter presage those of chapter 6. In chapter 6, I provide an overview of other intellectual changes that were occurring in criminal justice generally, and explore their impact on American policing. More specifically, I review the work of the American Bar Foundation and its "discovery" of discretion in criminal justice agencies, and revisit *The Challenge of Crime in a Free Society* and its role in creating an integrated systems approach to criminal justice. The cynicism that resulted in the themes discussed in this chapter and the proceeding chapter created an incredible anomic sentiment among police officers that, too, would need to be resolved by important organizational changes that resonate in the 21st century. To begin this discussion, I briefly review Packer's crime control and due process models, and then consider their application to the 1950s and 1960s criminal justice system, including the police.

PACKER'S DUAL-TAXONOMY MODEL

Packer outlined his criminal justice models in his now, sadly, somewhat forgotten 1968 volume *The Limits of the Criminal Sanction*. Most criminal justice students will only ever be introduced to Packer's writings via their textbooks, which provide an impression of the *crime control* and *due process* models that are somewhat watered down (for an exception, see Samuel Walker's publication, now in its 8th edition, *Sense and Nonsense about Crime, Drugs, and Community*). The purpose behind his models is clarified in the title of his 1968 book: the *limits* of the criminal sanction. Early in the book Packer makes the argument that while the world assumed that the justice system functioned according to systematic and constitutional guidelines, the truth was that very few people went through the entire criminal justice process as outlined by statutes and case law, and that not all crimes were treated equally in the eyes of the law. To 21st century eyes, this is no surprise; but for the *body politic* in the 1960s, this was dire news. Packer was not the first person to note that the justice system did not function as designed. As I'll discuss in the next chapter, the "discovery" of the discretion that criminal justice actors exercised in the 1950s would lead not only to the systems approach to criminal justice, but also to a host of theoretical work trying to explain how and why justice actors employed their discretion to *not* administer the law. But Packer's work, like Martinson's in the 1970s (the infamous and also largely misunderstood "nothing works" doctrine), would have widespread ramifications for criminal justice practitioners and scholars.

Packer's book pointed out a number of inconsistencies, both in terms of the way the system ought to work and the way that it did work, and in terms of the way people *thought* the system was working and the way that it did work. He boiled people's perceptions of how the justice system functioned into two camps—the crime control and due process models. Both models explain perceived behavior through the lenses of the interlocutor's values. Importantly, Packer conceived of these values as being in competition, resulting in a taxonomy that was polar rather than complementary. Both the crime control and due process models, however, were based on three similar assumptions:

- laws should define what behavior was criminal before defining how those convicted of crimes should be treated;
- the accused can and ought to be involved in the entire process of the administration of justice;
- and, ultimately, criminal justice agents should be enforcing the law, not providing social services.

These similarities are important for what they say about Packer's models. Namely, both are grounded in the American constitution and democratic ideals. This would matter insofar as the political confrontation that would ensue between the police—who were stalwart adopters of the crime control model—and other criminal justice actors, agencies, and politicians—who, largely driven by the scientific community and the Warren Court, were "experimenting" with the due process model—would be resolvable, in the end, thanks to these core values which both models held in common.

Those who subscribe to the *crime control model* want the justice system to be as *efficient* as possible. What this means practically is that due process is curtailed in favor of the swift execution of the law. This is not to say that due process is ignored, only that it does not take center stage, as we will see it does for the aptly named due process model. One of the reasons that the crime control model can dilute due process, conceptually, is because it focuses on what Packer describes as factual (as opposed to legal) guilt. Factual guilt is understood to be the "fact" that someone is, indeed, literally responsible for the actual illegal act, and is therefore rendered culpable. To a degree, factual guilt plays little part in American jurisprudence. Rather, the prosecuting attorney's purpose is to prove beyond a reasonable doubt all five elements of a crime (ie., *mens rea, actus reus*, concurrence, harm, and intent). Although one could argue that *actus reus* is factual guilt, one would be incorrect in doing so, insofar as the factual existence of *actus reus* is not what the courts ask of the prosecutor—it is only that the *actus reus* be proven beyond a reasonable doubt. The crime control model finds the concept of legal guilt somewhat of a fairy tale that lets real criminals off on technical details (although research reveals this to hardly be the case, see Walker, 2011).

In opposition to the crime control model is Packer's due process model. If the crime control model has been described as having an extreme focus on the efficient administration of the law, the due process model has been described as a legal obstacle course. In a due process model, efficiency is synonymous with railroading, which is simply another way to describe circumventing individual rights. For those who subscribe to the due process model, the power of the state over the individual is basically infinite, and therefore must be curtailed lest the individual suffer unduly. To this end, in order to convict, and therefore sanction a suspect/defendant, the state must overcome a series of procedural tests, each with their own evidentiary threshold. The burden of passing these tests is wholly on the state, and they are not at all easy or quick. Rather, they are deliberate and, by design, cumbersome. In this way, the due process model attempts to assure that only those who are truly guilty of their crime are actually punished. In American jurisprudence, *punishment* is best understood as the removal of liberties. And as the United States Constitution and its various amendments provide, whenever the state wants to abridge the rights and liberties of *any* person on American soil, they must do so according to due process.

The due process model takes William Blackstone's famous formulation, "It is better that ten guilty persons escape than that one innocent suffer," with utter seriousness. For the due process model, a suspect's/defendant's innocence is always assumed until proven otherwise beyond a reasonable doubt.

This is in contrast to what Packer describes as the crime control model's assumption of guilt. Understanding these assumptions is paramount for grasping the key distinctions between the crime control and due process models. The assumption of guilt to which the crime control model subscribes is not so much a cynical or even unconstitutional assumption, *per se*. Rather, it is an exceedingly practical assumption. The logic goes that if a person was arrested on probable cause, and if several magistrates also found probable cause that that person is culpable, there is most likely enough evidence that this person did, indeed, factually commit the crime for which he is accused. The due process model's assumption of innocence does not necessarily disagree with this line of reasoning, it simply doesn't care on philosophical and jurisprudential grounds. Philosophically, the assumption of innocence is seminal in due process thinking, and is the result of centuries of the abuse of Western European state power against innocent persons. Jurisprudentially, the assumption of innocence is not so much a literal assumption, as is the crime control model's assumption of guilt, but a legal heuristic tied up in the concept not of factual guilt but of legal guilt. Legally, American law does not really care if someone did or did not commit a crime—only that the elements of a crime can be proven beyond a reasonable doubt in an impartial and adversarial court. If the prosecutor is able to do so, then that person is presumed guilty and can be sanctioned—but such guilt is only a legal reality, and may or may not be grounded in factual reality.

This is often a very difficult concept for lay people to grasp, and it chafes against common sense and notions of fair-play. Many politicians and criminal justice practitioners are also not great fans of legal guilt over factual guilt. This is reflected in many legislative reforms, starting in the 1980s, that have bent the justice system toward a more crime control orientation, including an emphasis on victims and factual guilt. For example, just as the law cares little for factual guilt, it technically cares little for the factual victim. Under the social contract, when one breaks the law—even if one commits a personal crime against an actual person—it is the state which is considered the victim. This is reflected in the convention of recording court cases as "The State v." or "The people v.", etc. In such a system, the victim's place is best described as "evidence." In the 1980s (and continuing today), the victim began taking on a more active role in the court process, including being able to influence the sanctioning decision through victim-impact statements. But to take these contemporary moods and practice and project them onto the 1950s and 1960s is fallacious—one must keep historical context at the forefront. The Civil Rights Movement brought the abuses of the state to the forefront of the American psyche, and the Warren Court was making the due process model a reality, not just a philosophy. At a time when the entire nation seemed to be adopting a due process perception of what the justice system *should* be doing, the American police were (and still are) remaining staunchly crime control in what they perceived to be the purpose of the justice system.

Crime Control and the Police

Although there is substantial disagreement on the existence of a police "working personality"—or of what such a personality would consist (cf. Twersky-Glasner, 2005)—most surveys support the suggestion that police officers are, by and large, *conservative*, in both senses of that term. That is, police are conservative in the political sense, either as Republicans, Libertarians, or moderate-leaning-conservative Independents, and conservative in the sense that they eschew and distrust change. This characteristic was first described by Jerome Skolnick in his 1966 book *Justice without Trial* and then fully developed in his 1977 publication "A Sketch of the Policeman's 'Working Personality.'" As Skolnick noted in both publications, the conservativism of the police working personality facilitated the us-versus-them attitude of the police and the isolation of the police from those whom they supposedly served: While the public was moving toward a more liberal approach to social control, the police were unwilling to budge, increasing the social distance between them. This isolation and unwillingness to adequately adapt was aggravated by the bureaucratic nature of the police agency as designed under the professionalism of August Vollmer. The closed-model organization of the police bureaucracy, as has been pointed out in prior chapters, is by design uninterested in its environment and therefore unadaptable to it. One can say that the propensity to avoid change is built into the DNA of the police and their organization.

Like most conservatives, police believe that due process, while important, can be taken to extremes. These extremes can lead to irrational decisions that, in the end, hurt any effort to control crime. Police could argue that that sort of a scenario would lead not only to an increase in crime, but a decrease in public order (Walker, 2011). Under a crime control model, anything that hurts efficiency harms effectiveness, and this is contrary to the assumed purpose of the criminal justice system (as both Burke [2011] and Kraska [2006] point out, this is only *one* purpose of the criminal justice system—depending on how one conceptualizes the administration of justice, its "purpose" can be fluid). As the Warren Court began articulating case law that enforced police due process, police officers responded with the cry that the courts were "handcuffing" their ability to enforce the law and control crime. Although a handful of research flatly denies that this has been the result (Walker, 2011), the fact that it was (and is) perceived to be the case among police officers is what matters. The conservative nature of police and policing can be attested to by any introductory textbook, numerous articles, and in earlier chapters of this book. What matters for our current conversation is to place this conservatism in its historical context—that is, against a rising liberal response to crime coupled with newly enforced due process requirements.

The Push for Due Process and the Call for Rehabilitation

As I have already outlined in detail in chapter 3, starting in the 1950s and extending well into the 1960s, the American court system would concern itself heavily with due process. The courts, especially the federal courts, had, of course, done so a generation earlier, with such cases as *Weeks v. The United States* in 1914. The Warren Court, however, took the application of due process to a whole new level by incorporating many of those federal due process requirements previously outlined in case law to the states, generally by way of the 14th Amendment. The courts would continue to take a special interest in due process, particularly where the police were concerned, well into the 1980s and throughout the 1990s. These later changes were not as revolutionary as those implemented by the Warren Court, however—hence Graham's (1970) book, *The Due Process Revolution*, and its telling subtitle, *The Warren Court's Impact on Criminal Law.* Due process case law under the Rehnquist Court of the 1980s and 1990s can better be understood as a refining of the legal pronouncements handed down by the Warren Court. (Or, if one wants to put a cynical, but perhaps no less accurate, spin on things, the Rehnquist Court's actions can also be understood as a slow but deliberate chipping away of the civil rights codified in case law under the Warren Court; cf. Schwartz, 2002). One can understand the actions of the Warren Court, therefore, as putting the ideals of what Packer describes as a due process model of criminal justice into practice: maintaining all burdens on the government, while protecting the suspect/defendant—assumed to be innocent—with a gauntlet of hoops through which the government must jump in order to deny that person's liberties.

Police received these case laws as if they were a personal blow to their professionalism. They felt that the new case law was "handcuffing" their ability to fight crime. If we take Packer's dual taxonomy model as a starting point, the police were, in fact, correct: the due process model is not concerned with efficiency—rather, it is concerned with making things "tough" on the government, to balance things out. The due process model recognizes the awesome and, in comparison to the civilian, infinite power of the state, and does its best to equal the playing field. Further, the due process and crime control models understand "effectiveness" differently—whereas both are concerned with catching the bad guy and reducing/preventing crime, the due process model also refuses to take it on faith that if a suspect is able to be found guilty via probable cause throughout all stages of the process, then that person is *ipso facto* guilty. Thus, the due process model has the added measurements of effectiveness of making sure that an innocent person is *not* found guilty, *and* making sure that *all* suspects/defendants are not railroaded by the justice system.

By and large, one can reasonably ascribe the due process model to liberals, just as one can safely ascribe the crime control model to conservatives. Prior to the 1960s (and the introduction of the systems model of criminal justice), this meant that any liberal interference with the police was felt through politics alone. Interference may have had an actual impact on the day to day behavior of the police, but in the end it was lumped together with other trite complaints about those with whom anyone or any party might disagree. To a degree, therefore, the police were able to continue in their conservative, crime control, professional model. Not so in the 1960s, now that the police were no longer just "the police" but were part of the "criminal justice *system*." As part of the system, the police had to learn to play well with others, something that they were not used to doing. While the next chapter explores these interactions in more depth, it is important at this juncture to note that the newly christened criminal justice "system" was moving in *one* direction, while the police were moving in another direction—or, better stated, the police were maintaining their current position with reckless stubbornness that even George Patton could appreciate.

The new direction of the criminal justice system was not only based on liberal due process ideals, but on liberal ideas about rehabilitation (Walker, 2011). Both were undergirded by the federal courts, the one under the constitution (due process) and the other under the concept of government accountability for those who became "wards"—one way or another—of the state (rehabilitation). The idea was this: if the state has taken the initiative to hold someone against that person's will, in such a way as to have near total control over that person's life, then it is the state's responsibility to care for that individual. In one sense, this rehabilitative ideal harkened back to the Quakers of Pennsylvania and their brand of incarcerated isolation, with nothing but a small trade and a Bible, in the hope that labor and the Good Word would cure and save a soul—and make for a better person once they came back to society. The mid-twentieth century's resurrection of rehabilitation was, however, very different from that of the Quakers. For one, it was at least conceptualized to be personalized to the prisoner. For another, it was essentially stripped of any religiosity. Instead, the focus was on addiction recovery, learning technical skills, and overcoming anti-social habits. One thing that both the Quakers and prison reformers of the 20th century did have in common in their approach to incarceration, however, was that rehabilitation, not punishment, was the point of incarceration. Prison was *not* a place one went to be punished—prison was a place where one went to become a person who is able and willing to contribute to society—to become, as the word rehabilitation itself suggests, part of the norm (Walker, 1998).

Rehabilitation assumes some very key principles about human beings: that they are teachable, and that they are at their core good persons. This went against what most police felt about those who committed crimes. "Criminals" were scumbags and assholes (Van Maanen, 1978) who didn't change. If someone got caught committing a crime, they were most assuredly guilty of dozens of other offenses. Prisons were meant to, and could only be, a place of pain and punishment. Rehabilitation, however, would be backed up by the courts, if not directly then at least in principle through a series of court cases affirming the dignity of prisoners. This was done primarily by the courts by setting standards designed to reduce the abuse of prisoners and to create accountability mechanisms for prisons (Walker, 1998).

As Walker (2011) outlines in his *Sense and Nonsense* chapter aptly titled "Treat 'em!", these liberal ideals were just that—ideals. The idealism of the liberal urge to rehabilitate would be blunted by Robert Martinson's 1974 article "What Works? Questions and Answers about Prison Reform." In this article, Martinson famously stated that, "with few and isolated exceptions, the rehabilitative efforts that have been reported so far have had no appreciable effect on rehabilitation" (p. 25). Martinson's statement was based on a review of over two hundred scientific studies on treatment programs across over 20 years. Of those, a majority—52 percent—did not "work". But as one can see from Martinson's own statement, clearly some (48 percent) *must* have worked (and the debate continues on what "working" really means in this context). But by the 1970s, the tide was already turning away from the liberal approach to crime control (Walker, 1998), and in a way Martinson's article (and subsequent book) put the nail in rehabilitation's coffin. By now, the "get tough on crime" mantra was getting revved up, only to be in full swing a decade later (and forever onward after that). Conservatives capitalized and cherry-picked Martinson's report, and thus was born the idea that, when it comes to rehabilitation, "nothing works." This accusation, although inaccurate, can hardly be applied to liberal approaches uniquely.

THE RISE OF THE NEW CYNICISM

We should not be surprised that Martinson's findings were, in the very least, discouraging regarding rehabilitation. The rehabilitative fervor of the 1950s and 1960s is guilty of the same behavior as the police during this time period: Assuming that the etiology of crime, and therefore society's response to it, was simple. Responses would become more appropriately nuanced in the latter 20th century up into the present. These changes will be explored in the ninth and final chapter. But while police may have maintained their doubts about the effectiveness (and justness) of due process and rehabilitation, they were a political reality which which they had to live. To borrow a Biblical image, they could only kick against the goads for so long. And even in the 1970s, the demise of the rehabilitation model, ushered to its grave as it was through the empirical work of Martinson and others, was hardly unique to the liberal approach to crime control. Both patterns were part of what Walker (2015) describes as the *new cynicism*.

The new cynicism was non-partisan in its effects—both conservatives and liberals were "fed up" with the newly donned justice system, but for different reasons. For conservatives, the concern was that irrational decision making, as a consequence of new criminal justice due process, was leading to ineffective crime control. For liberals, the entire system was seen as one of chaos that penalized the poor and minorities because it was, at its core, discriminatory. The new cynicism can therefore be characterized by a universal frustration with the operations and outcomes of all criminal justice agencies—including the police. Those who expressed this new cynicism came from all parts of society: politicians, civilians, and even the justice actors, themselves—again, including the police. According to Walker (2015), it replaced what he labeled as the "old idealism." Under the old idealism, it was believed that all criminal justice actors did what they were supposed to do the way they were supposed to do it. For example, the police were supposed to arrest on probable cause and were to treat the suspect according to due process. As Americans would soon discover, however, this was far from the reality. The fall of the old idealism and its consequences is taken up in the next chapter. Under the new cynicism, the Pollyanna-like trust in the administration of justice and the administrators of justice was replaced with distrust, disillusionment, righteous outrage, and no small amount of fear. Broad and universal reform was in the air.

The new cynicism was bolstered by new research. And just as research would topple rehabilitation, so too would it debunk some of the most loudly voiced concerns of the police and conservatives regarding the due process revolution. The biggest concern was that the exclusionary rule and the *Miranda* warnings would "lose" guilty persons on technicalities. This was simply not the case, however. For example, Schulhofer (1998) found that *Miranda* had practically no impact on police effectiveness, and Fyfe (1983) found similar results for the exclusionary rule. This was not because police were not abiding by the court's rulings. Rather, it was because the court's rulings had little impact on *what* the police did (although there is some evidence that they did impact *how* the police did these things [see Orfield, 1987]—surely the enduring cinematic value of the *Miranda* warnings testify to this). Police cases—and hence prosecutors' cases—are made and broken by eyewitness testimony and confessions. One of those—eyewitness testimony—does not rely on the exclusionary rule nor does it rely on *Miranda*, and the other—confessions—are often offered *in spite of Miranda* warnings. Indeed, it is not uncommon that the suspect turns himself in. Further, it is most often the case that crimes are committed against a victim who knows the perpetrator, thus greasing the wheels of due process, so to speak. As I have been stressing throughout this book, however, it is not the empirical reality of the effects of the due process revolution (or anything else) that matter—it was what that revolution, in tandem with other social changes in crime "control," meant to the police.

CONCLUSIONS

If these things—rehabilitation, due process, crime fighting, etc.—really "didn't matter," then an important question is begged: did they have any impact whatsoever on the police? The answer is a firm *yes*. So much of what the police do is symbolic—and so much of what the public expects the police to do is also largely symbolic (Crank, 2004). This has been most eloquently explored by Manning (1977), borrowing heavily from Goffman's famous work on symbolic interactionism and the idea of dramaturgy. The basic question before any police organization is *what we are supposed to accomplish?* Under the professionalism of August Vollmer, the answer was *to fight crime and thereby make the world a safer place.* As part of Vollmer's bureaucratizing movement, the police isolated themselves from a number of organizations who might have assisted them in this goal. In doing so, they signed their own death warrant. As Herbert (2001) put it, "...on their own, police can do little to reduce crime" (p. 449). I would amend this statement with the prefix: "Under the professional model and left to their own devices..." The police therefore had to resort to a number of ways to "symbolically" represent their success and status as *the* professional crime fighters, or, as Manning (1977) wrote, police had to engage in the "dramatic management of the appearance of effectiveness" (p. 20). We have already seen how the police did this: by implementing and encouraging a 911 system; by being at the forefront of technology, including two way radios and fingerprints; and in a massive public relations campaign that was largely spearheaded by the FBI, but also by some local law enforcement agencies, such as the Los Angeles Police Department's involvement with the 1950s drama *Dragnet* (Hayde, 2001; Webb, 2005).

But all this came to a crumbling halt in the 1960s. Faced with a turn in the political tides—from a conservative, crime control model to a more liberal, due process model—on both the social and professional level, the police were left alone. What's worse, they were now part of a "system" which expected them to come along with the tide. The police, at first and over several decades, simply refused—but with federal pressures, such refusal was certainly perfunctory. Change was coming—as we have seen, especially so in the form of federal monies. In the mean time, they felt the pangs of ostracization from all ends. The impact of this soup of distrust and polarizing positions on crime control had to have been felt by the police throughout the nation—and it certainly manifested itself in what Niederhoffer (1969) would describe as professional cynicism. Others, too, would document police officer malaise with the state of their profession during this time period (Rubinstein, 1973).

The malaise was compounded by the fact that the crime rate was rising, as were police calls for service. So as police were receiving the message, *you're doing things all wrong, you're out of sync*, they were simultaneously receiving the message, *we need you, and we need you now more than ever*. This macro-level cognitive dissonance would reach a breaking point over the next twenty years, finally forcing out not only the old idealism but the new cynicism. The result would be what some have called the *new* criminal justice. First, though, police would have to endure the sudden shift to the "systems" model of criminal justice, in tandem with the utter destruction of the old idealism.

Chapter Six

The Systems Approach to Criminal Justice

At several points thus far in this book, and particularly over the last two chapters, I have made mention of the "new" systems approach to understanding the role of and relationship between those agencies charged with the administration of law in the United States. This is an important topic to consider, as it revolutionized just how such agencies framed their quotidien work—as well as changed how politicians and civilians conceptualized the purpose and nature of these agencies. No longer did one think of the "police" in a vacuum—now one thought of the "criminal justice system." Several things occurred to make this a reality, most notably the publication of the President's Crime Commission's *The Challenge of Crime in a Free Society*, the development of which I have already discussed over the last two chapters. The commission was largely influenced by the systems theory in vogue at that time among organizational theorists, and which was having an impact across both the political and private sphere. This might explain *why* police were thrown into a newly conceived "justice system," but the reason why such a change was even perceived as necessary was heralded by a number of other factors, many of which we have already considered. For example, the rising crime rate and frightening increase in race riots aimed at the police surely contributed to the notion that *something* needed to change in how we understood the role of the justice system.

Before change could occur, however, it was necessary to understand just *how*, in fact, the police, courts, and correctional agencies were behaving. As Supreme Court Justice Robert Jackson apocryphally noted, "No one really knows just how the criminal law system is working or what its defects really are." This statement resulted in yet another event that, so far, I have only mentioned in passing: a survey conducted by the American Bar Foundation on criminal justice agencies nationwide. This survey's impact on the po-lice—and, indeed, on the justice system as a whole—cannot be understated. Not only did the ABF survey "blow the lid" off the regular use of discretion in law enforcement (and in other justice agencies), it demonstrated the rela-tionship between the component parts that would later be tied together under the "systems" model. This approach would add a whole new level of ac-countability to the police and further fuel the sense that they were alone—not only among the body politic, but among the entire "system". The most imme-diate impact of the ABF's survey, however, was the absolute destruction of the old idealism, and the introduction of the new cynicism (Walker, 2015).

Combined, the ABF survey and *The Challenge of Crime in a Free Society* hurdled police toward their own brand of cynicism. The entire world seemed against them: the people were rioting against them, politicians were blaming them, the courts were handcuffing them, and now the federal government was dictating anew the form and function of their profession that was largely based on a due process model. Police palpably felt that they were no longer the solution to the crime problem. Now, they were considered part of a larger social problem. This anomic feeling would express itself as professional cynicism and pessimism, and sometimes as a moral form of corruption (as opposed to an economic form of corruption) given the name by DeLattre (see his 2006 edition) and popularized by John Crank and Michael Caldero (2000) as *noble cause corruption*. Perhaps the ethos of noble cause corrup-tion and the general sentiment of the police in regard to the criminal justice system is best summed up with an appeal to popular media, specifically, a conversation between veteran detective Lester and rookie Sydnor on the HBO series *The Wire* (cf. Cooper & Bolen, 2013):

> Lester: "I've reached a point, Detective Sydnor, where I no longer have the time or patience left to address myself to the needs of the system within which we work. I'm tired."
> Sydnor: "You gonna quit?"
> Lester: "Not yet. Not just yet."
> Sydnor: "So what are you talking about?"
> Lester: "[When they took us off Marlo,] I regarded that decision as illegiti-mate...And so, I'm responding in kind. I'm going to press a case...without regard to the usual rules."

This chapter explores these themes, and makes the argument that the systems approach affected the police in ways that, if left unattended, would result in the implosion of American law enforcement. As with all other events I have so far covered in this book, change from *within* the police was necessary to prevent this outcome.

THE ABF SURVEY AND THE DISCOVERY OF DISCRETION

Walker (2015, see especially page 39) describes the state of America's understanding of the operations of the criminal justice apparatus prior to the 1960s as the "old idealism." He characterizes this old idealism as a "civic-book picture of justice". What Walker means by this description is that people believed that justice was administered formulaically, where "diligent and hardworking officials enforce the law as it is written in the statutes". Another way of saying this is that the administrators of justice never had agency when it came to their jobs—that they lacked choice. In the parlance of jurisprudence and justice research, they were believed to completely lack discretion. Nothing, however, could be further from the truth: "...this version of the criminal process does not describe the reality of our justice system" (p. 39). Walker is writing with almost half a century of hindsight. Prior to the 1960s, no one could have made such a statement with any degree of empirical surety. Indeed, the old idealism was just that: an *ideal*, not a positivist knowledge-base. It was this sort of naivety and ignorance that led Justice Jackson to bluntly point out that we, as a nation and, indeed, as justice actors, had no clue about what was (and was not) going on.

The American Bar Foundation decided to remedy this extreme lacunae in our knowledge of justice by undergoing the first nationwide survey of the behavior of justice agents. Their work was more than a "paper and pencil" survey—it also involved an incredible amount of systematic and direct social observation. Their study would result in numerous publications, including five in-house book length treatments of the data (Dawson's 1969 publication, *Sentencing;* LaFave's 1965 publication, *Arrest: The Decision to Take a Suspect into Custody*; Miller's 1969 publication, *Prosecution: The Decision to Charge a Suspect with a Crime*; Newman's 1966 publication, *Conviction: The Determination of Guilt or Innocence without Trial*; and Tiffany, McIntyre, and Rotenberg's 1966 publication, *Detection of Crime: Stopping and Questioning, Search and Seizure, Encouragement and Entrapment*), and a host of independent study publications, such as Goldstein's (1960) powerfully influential *Police Discretion Not to Invoke the Criminal Process*. These titles say it all: "The staff [of the ABF research team] was astonished at the pervasive exercise of discretion, the extent to which it was unregulated, and the often conflicted purposes it served" (Walker, 1998, p. 203; see also Walker, 1992).

Arguably the two areas of research that have most been affected by the ABF survey and its "discovery" of discretion in the administration of justice have been the courts (for a detailed understanding of the role of discretion in sentencing decisions, see any of the numerous publications on this subject written or co-authored by Cassia Spohn) and the police. For the police, this was in part because, as Corsianos (2003) points out, they work within a complex social framework where independent decision making is necessary. The fact that it is necessary does not preclude problems, however—born largely of the fact that police discretion typically occurs outside the bounds of supervision (although this is changing to an incredible extent with new cell phone technology, that is, camera phones, and with dash and shoulder cameras becoming more commonly assigned to police officers). Discretion is the result of the *legal powers* that police officers hold, the *act of enforcing the criminal law*, and the *context* of police work, including the public yet largely unsupervised nature of people work that limits direct control over their behavior [cf. McLaughlin and Muncie (2001)]. The result, as uncovered by the ABF and innumerable subsequent research, was that police often use their authority with no legal basis.

Even outside the social context of the 1960s, this situation is rife with potentially damaging effects. It begs a question that, prior to the ABF survey, would not have even dawned on the public, politicians, or researchers: if not legal reasons, then what would influence an officer to make an arrest, or do anything? By definition, these had to be extra-legal reasons, which is simply another way of saying illegal reasons. As I have noted elsewhere (see Cooper, 2014, especially pages 24 and 25):

> At the individual level, we have an idea that departmental policy (Fyfe, 1982), personal background, and suspect demeanor (Smith, 1981), among others, have some impact on how an officer behaves. At higher levels of aggregation, such as the precinct or agency, we believe that the political climate of the city (Wilson, 1968; Chappell, 2006), demographic characteristics of their service area (Kane, 2002), and the areal based work group (Klinger, 1997) all influence police behavior. (p. 1)

There is also uncomfortable but ample evidence that the race of the suspect and her community also influence police officer behavior (Rojek, Rosenfeld, & Decker, 2012; Rice & White, 2010). Simply stated, African American suspects are more likely to be stopped, frisked, interrogated, arrested, and have force used against them than their White counterparts, net of controls (Walker, Spohn, & Delone, 2012). Clearly, this sort of behavior on the part of the police added to the racial fervor I covered in chapter four.

The immediate result of the ABF survey and its finding that justice actors behaved with discretion that, to a large degree, was uninhibited, was a complete dismantling of the old idealism. It was to be replaced by what Walker (2015) calls the "new cynicism". Contrary to the *Dragnet*-like image of policing proffered by the old idealism, the new cynicism viewed the entire administration of justice as chaotic, and believed that police discretion was completely out of control. Walker breaks the new cynicism down into two camps, one for conservatives and the other for liberals. For conservatives, the new cynicism was compounded by their view that justice was being administered under a due process, as opposed to a crime control, model (more on this below). This, they believed, only added to the chaos by leading to a number of irrational "technical" decisions that ultimately undermined crime control. Liberals, on the other hand, while applauding the seemingly due process direction of the courts under Earl Warren, still believed that not only was there discrimination within the system, but that the system itself was discriminatory. Either way, the rose-colored-glass view of the justice system that existed prior to the 1950s was no more: it was now believed to be an entropic mess that was ineffective and racist.

The new cynicism's dual conservative and liberal viewpoints set up a dichotomy in terms of how aggressive the police were: either they were too lenient or they were too severe. This dichotomy, however, was completely false: "Norval Morris and Michael Tonry argue that... 'We are both too lenient and too severe.' This paradox is key to understanding how our criminal justice system really works" (Walker, 2015, p. 41). So even after the ABF survey, there was widespread misunderstanding and simplification concerning the form and function of the criminal justice system, including the police.

In some respects, however, the new cynicism was justified. For one, and as I have already covered, research—both that from the ABF report and others that followed the several publications resulting from the ABF's survey—consistently showed that not only were police *not* doing what they were supposed to do, but what they were doing (including when they did do what they were supposed to do) was embarrassingly ineffective. But more so, the ABF survey vindicated minority communities who had for decades been crying out about the abuse they experienced—not just at the hands of the police, but at all levels of the justice system. Their story was what the ABF found: police did not follow due process and used an enormous amount of discretion, largely to the detriment of minority neighborhoods *because* they were minority neighborhoods. Then came the blue ribbon commissions which reinforced this minority viewpoint. *Something* had to change. The federal government's answer, as articulated in the *Challenge of Crime in a Free Society* report, was a reframing of the purpose and form of all apparati involved in the administration of justice.

THE SYSTEMS APPROACH: CONTENT

The task before the President's Commission in describing the criminal justice system was more daunting them some might imagine. In their opening introductory chapter, under the section titled "America's System of Criminal Justice," they write:

> The system of criminal justice America uses to deal with those crimes it cannot prevent and those criminals it cannot deter is not a monolithic, or even

a consistent, system. It was not designed or built in one piece at one time. Its philosophic core is that a person may be punished by the Government if, and only if, it has been proved by an impartial and deliberate process that he has violated a specific law. Around that core layer upon layer of institutions and procedures, some carefully constructed and some improvised, some inspired by principle and some by expediency, have accumulated. Parts of the system—magistrates' courts, trial by jury, bail—are of great antiquity. Other parts—juvenile courts, probation and parole, professional policemen—are relatively new. The entire system represents an adaptation of the English common law to America's peculiar structure of government, which allows each local community to construct institutions that fill its special needs. *Every village, town, county, city, and State has its own criminal justice system, and there is a Federal one as well. All of them operate somewhat alike. No two of them operate precisely alike.* (p. 7, emphasis mine)

Despite this challenge, the President's Commission made a courageous effort to describe the administration of justice as a system. The most memorable manner that they accomplished this was through *the* flowchart, which was printed at the start of the President's Commission's report on pages 8 and 9. As the report itself indicated, the purpose of the flowchart was to "present a simple yet comprehensive view of the movement of cases through the criminal justice system." As important as the flowchart was (and is), however, the flowchart itself was merely a result of what the report demonstrated. Basically, the flowchart was the graphical representation of what *Challenge of Crime in a Free Society* called *decision points*: particular moments in the criminal justice system where discretion was available, either *de jure* or *de facto*. The "discovery" of these decision points replicated what the ABF found in their own survey, namely the inaccuracy of the old idealism. But it went one step further:

> The popular, or even the lawbook, theory of everyday criminal process oversimplifies in some respects and overcomplicates in others what usually happens...Some cases do proceed much like that, especially those involving offenses that are generally considered "major": serious acts of violence or thefts of large amounts of property. However, not all major cases follow this course, and, in any event, the bulk of the daily business of the criminal justice system consists of offenses that are not major—of breaches of the peace, crimes of vice, petty thefts, assaults arising from domestic or street-corner or barroom dispute. These and most other cases are disposed of in much less formal and much less deliberate ways. (p. 7)

The systems approach, as applied to agencies charged with the administration of justice, demonstrated how each agency had its own task to execute, but at the same time, that each agency was not, in fact, independent. Rather, what one agency did inevitably impacted the decision points—and therefore the outcomes—of what other agencies would do. This, as we will see in a moment, had profound ramifications for the police. The report described the usefulness and purpose of conceptualizing the administration of justice as a system in three terms (see page 54 of the report): to reveal the underlying assumptions of the system; to facilitate experimentation; and to identify data needed to explore proposed changes. Klofas (2010) boils these down to understanding "how [the justice system] works...how it might change...what data are needed to estimate the impact of any change in one component on other parts of the system" (p. 17).

But the systems approach also had something to say about how the suspect was treated by this new justice system, as well. (Note that it said very little about the victim—that would not occur until the 1980s; cf. Bostaph and Cooper, 2007). Indeed, the flowchart demonstrated how the *suspect* moved throughout the justice system, and how various decision points affected his chances of what the report called "diversion": opportunities, as dictated by the system, to avoid the full measure of the administration of justice. Some of these opportunities were informal, such as a police officer just letting someone go, quasi-formal, such as plea bargains, and absolutely formal, such as a judge handing down an acquittal. Regardless, this focus on the *suspect's* movement *through* the system was indicative of the systems approach's basic assumptions (read: due process) about the purpose of the criminal justice system: "Our system of justice deliberately sacrifices much in efficiency and even in effectiveness in order to preserve local autonomy and to protect the individual" (p. 7). What this quote indicates is that, at its heart, the systems approach espouses the values of the *due process model*. Importantly, however, it did recognize the reality and necessity of crime control:

> In the interest both of effectiveness and of fairness to individuals, justice should be swift and certain; too often in city courts today it is, instead, hasty or faltering. Invisibly, the pressure of numbers has effected a series of adventurous changes in the criminal process. Informal shortcuts have been used. The decision making process has often become routinized. Throughout the system the importance of individual judgment and discretion, as distinguished from stated rules and procedures, has increased. In effect, much decision making is being done on an administrative rather than on a judicial basis. (p. 8)

The report then went on to recognize the unknown quantity of discretion that characterized the justice system: "Thus, an examination of how the criminal justice system works and a consideration of the changes needed to make it more effective and fair must focus on the extent to which invisible, administrative procedures depart from visible, traditional ones, and on the desirability of that departure" (p. 8).

Discretion and the New Justice System

In *Popular Justice*, Walker (1998) opines: "without any question, the Commission's most significant and lasting contribution was its 'systems' model of the criminal justice system" (p. 203). I tend to agree with such a strong and unequivocal statement. But why? For one, the systems approach "...emphasized dynamic relationships among police, court, and correctional agencies and the critical role of discretionary decision making in determining whether cases were sent forward or removed from the system" (p. 203). Two important changes resulted because of this emphasis. First, and as I've pointed out, we understood for the first time the relationship between the decisions made by various criminal justice agencies on other criminal justice agencies. Secondly, was the emergence of a new avenue for incredibly diverse and fruitful criminal justice research exploring the nature of discretion in the justice system. This research ascertained both the frequency and importance of discretion in the justice system. Although it could be abused, its necessity could also be controlled or, at least, directed. In a sense, discretion can be understood as the legally granted authority to choose how to act in any given situation within procedural and jurisdictional guidelines.

This body of research explored the role and nature of discretion throughout all justice agencies. Regarding police, for example, Black and Reiss (1970) discovered that patrol officers did not always make arrests even when probable cause was apparent. For courts, Eisenstein and Jacob (1977) discovered how discretion within the courtroom work group allowed for a political process to govern how some felony cases were handled apart from the traditional adversarial process [what Walker (2015) referred to as the "going rate"]. And for prisons, Goffman (1961) laid the groundwork for understanding how discretion was used to create working relations between guards and prisoners in order to maintain a predictable and operable correctional facility. Each of these studies revealed how discretion underpinned the entire criminal justice system, while simultaneously undermining many of its ideals.

Research also revealed the etiology of discretion. For the police, there were at least three sources of discretion. As with most social phenomena, these sources are interrelated, yet distinct enough to discuss independently. The three sources were: the nature of the work, the influence of professionalism, the organizational structure, and policing innovations.

The Nature of the Work. It has been suggested that the very nature of police work necessitates a high degree of discretion. Indeed, the discretion involved in police work varies from the decision to stop a speeding vehicle to the decision to take a life (Fyfe, 1986; Van Maanen, 1974). The necessity of discretion lies in the fact that most of what police do is accomplished outside the purview of official supervision (Corsianos, 2003), and often takes place privately rather than publicly (Gottfredson & Gottfredson, 1988). The ability to hold police officers accountable *in real time* has been a constant struggle since the inception of the modern police force in England under Sir Robert Peel at the start of the 19th century, and was a topic that plagued police reformist August Vollmer (Uchida, 2005; Walker, 1998). It is this private, discretionary nature that renders accountability for officers so difficult (Walker, 2005).

Brooks (2005) correctly pointed out that not all officers will act with the same level of discretion all of the time: discretion is situational and governed by context. While the nature of police work provided the situational element necessary for discretion to occur, research suggested that professionalism and the organizational structure provided the context.

The Influence of Professionalism. Professionalism has influenced policing since the early 1900s—and despite reform continues to influence the way the police conceive of and execute their duties (Uchida, 2005). To be a professional, among other things, suggests that a person is uniquely equipped to make decisions within her field of work. Vollmer, aided by Hoover's newly recreated FBI, pushed for the professionalization of policing and with it a mandate to fight crime (Manning, 1978; Uchida, 2005). Concomitant with this mandate was the title of "professional crime fighter". This meant that police considered themselves as skilled crime fighters uniquely set apart from citizens. As such, their actions were above public reproach (Walker, 2005). This created not only an opportunity for discretion, as explained by the nature of police work, but gave discretion professional and vocational meaning.

The Organizational Structure. The third source of discretion in police work is the organizational structure. Organizational structure refers to policies and practices unique to any given agency, as well as the complete collection of city codes and state statutes an officer is expected to enforce. Both Brooks (2005) and Corsianos (2003) have pointed out that laws are often vague or contradictory, therefore necessitating discretion on the part of an arresting officer. Similarly, they also pointed out that minor laws may, by common practice, not regularly be enforced. Ultimately, police are simply unable to always enforce all the laws for any given situation (Corsianos, 2003)—which requires discretion concerning *which* laws to enforce, as well as *where* and *when*. Often, agencies can indicate, formally or informally, which laws are to be enforced in which circumstances, and which laws can be left to the discretion of the officer. Fyfe (1979) demonstrated that an agency's policies can have an impact on discretionary choices, in this specific case with use of force policies (cf. Fyfe, 1982 for a comparison between New York City police shootings and those of Memphis in light of use of force policies).

The President's Commission's report would succeed in revolutionizing how the administration of justice was conceptualized, both in terms of the relationship between all of the agencies involved, and in terms of the sources, execution, and nature of discretion. But not all of its consequences were intended.

THE SYSTEMS APPROACH: CONSEQUENCES

In terms of the flowchart, police officer discretion can decide whether an individual will enter the criminal justice system at all. The most serious crimes tend to leave less discretion to police officers, whereas those that are less serious require more discretion on the part of the officer (Bittner, 1967; Litwin, 2004; Warner, 1997). Further, it has been found that police are more likely to invoke their law enforcement powers with misdemeanor or ticketable—that is, less serious—offenses when presented with an "asshole," or someone who unduly challenges their authority. Police see this not only as a challenge to themselves personally and collectively, but as a threat to public order (Van Maanen, 1978). What is more, they may ignore other offenses for the sake of going after a good "pinch" and doing "real" police work (Van Maanen, 1974).

Police officer discretion is consequential, both in terms of the daily practices of individual officers and the operations of agencies. Officer discretion that has resulted in unconstitutional or, at minimum, questionable outcomes has been the catalyst for a number of court cases that have curtailed police officer discretion. These cases include *Miranda v. Arizona* (1966) and *Mapp v. Ohio* (1961). Similarly, inappropriate use of force among police officers has resulted in a number of policies outlining when lethal force was appropriate (Fyfe, 1979; 1982; 1986). Finally, during the 1970s and 1980s, the use of discretion in regard to domestic violence was questioned by both conservative law and order advocates and liberal women rights advocates, resulting in a period of mandatory domestic violence arrest policies (Sherman & Berk, 1984; Sherman, 1992). These examples demonstrate that discretion not only plays a role in the day-to-day operations of police officers, but actually can have implications for how policing is itself structured and organized.

Officer discretion is also consequential in terms of an agency's relationship with citizens. Brooks (2005) has pointed out that discretion can exist at the both the individual officer level and at the administrative level. At the administrative level, discretion influences where to focus patrol efforts, training, hiring practices, and other similar tasks. This has had a significant impact both on the hiring of minority officers (Walker & Katz, 2011; White, 2007) and on selective enforcement (or non-enforcement) of minority neighborhoods (Reiss, 1971). One of the consequences for this latter use of police discretion has been poor relations with minority communities and individuals.

As has already been discussed, historically, police in the United States have had poor relations with members of minority and disadvantaged communities. This reality came to a head in the 1960s during the "long hot summers" of race riots (Walker, 1998) that culminated in a presidential commission that pointed a finger squarely at the police for being a major catalytic component to the riots (i.e., the Kerner Commission of 1968; cf. Walker, 1998). Minority citizens continue to tend to hold less favorable opinions of the police compared to Whites (Weitzer, 1999; Weitzer & Tuch, 2005; Weitzer, Tuch, & Skogan, 2008). Both Weitzer and Tuch (2005) and Weitzer, Tuch, and Skogan (2008) demonstrated that the opinions of minority citizens vis-à-vis the police as a whole are influenced by personal and vicarious experience with officers. For example, the latter study found that both traffic stops and pedestrian stops increased perceptions of police misconduct among African Americans. It was also found that when calls for service were handled in a professional manner, this served to increase African Americans' opinions of police officers. Both studies found that community oriented policing practices also increased African American citizens' opinions about the police. These studies suggest that the choices officers make during their interaction with citizens can have an important impact on the image the public holds of them. In turn, this can impact their legitimacy, hindering or helping them in their crime control efforts (Kane, 2005; Russell-Brown, 2009; Tyler, 2006).

The effect of discretion in the justice *system*, not just discretion among the police but throughout all criminal justice agencies, had a direct impact on the police themselves, in at least four related domains: the crystallization of the policing culture, as defined by an "us versus them" mentality and a "blue code of silence"; the rise (some might argue the return) of the distribution of "street justice" at the hands of patrol officers; the development of a moral, as opposed to an economic, form of police corruption that Ernest Hopkins first observed in his 1931 publication *Our Lawless Police* and that was later fully articulated by Michael Caldero and John Crank (1999) in *Police Ethics: The Corruption of Noble Cause* and Edwin DeLattre (2002) in *Character and Cops*, but which was also noted by such seminal policing scholars in the 1960s and 1970s as John Muir in his 1977 publication *Police: Streetcorner Politicians*; and an anomic occupational/worldview that manifested in intense cynicism. Each of these domains existed prior to the ABF's survey and the President's Commission—but the systems model of justice resulting from these reports intensified them to such an extent that they evolved from something normative to being seen as justifiably necessary for the police officer to meaningfully do his job.

The Police Culture

An enormous amount has been written concerning the culture of the police, far too much to cover in this book, let alone this chapter. But it was during the decades covered in this volume that a scholarly, as opposed to popular, understanding of police culture began to emerge. The popular image of the police, epitomized largely by the LAPD in *Dragnet*, was shattered as we began to understand that this culture was deeply flawed. Under the professional model, in tandem with the pre-systems understanding of the administration of justice, police could maintain a *Dragnet*-like facade. Once the problematic nature of the relationship between the police and minority communities became both a media and political issue, and the administration of justice was re-imagined as a *system* of justice, this facade fell apart like a house of cards (Strecher, 1971).

While it is accurate to portray the police culture of the 1950s, 1960s, and 1970s as being defined as "us versus them" (Kappeler, Sluder, & Alpert, 1998), it is important to note, as Strecher (1971) did during this era, that it is a culture based on social *roles*. The role of the police was seen by the police as utterly essential to the fabric of American society. As one officer quoted by Van Maanen (1974) put it, "You just can't give an honest picture of what happens in society without talking about what the cop on the street does" (p. 1). The *role* of the police was therefore to maintain social order by capturing the bad guy, and the role of civilians was to supply the bad guys. As Strecher (1971) also noted, interactions between police and civilians were based more on these social roles than on any single person's status as a unique individual. While this social shorthand may result in greater efficiency, it also resulted in increased stereotyping. And this cut both ways: civilians were just as likely to caricature police and respond to those caricatures rather than to the individual police officer. The net result was a social disconnect between the police and society:

> In general, there is little to link patrolmen to the private citizen in terms of establishing a socially satisfying relationship. Small businessmen have perhaps something to gain in terms of the protection a rapid response might provide. However, businessmen know that there is little likelihood that the patrolman they are friendly with today will respond to a call for help tomorrow. Similarly, patrolmen recognize accurately that few civilians are likely to return favors. For mutual concern and friendship to develop, some sort of exchange relationship must be sustained—[a] *quid pro quo*... In the police world, patrolmen rarely see the same people twice unless the contact is of the adversary variety. And such encounters are not apt to prove rewarding to the patrolman regarding the development of friendships. (Van Maanen, 1974, p. 103)

This disconnect would spill over into other agencies charged with the administration of justice, who had developed a culture that differed from that of the police. All this served to bring the police culture into closer contact with the civilian (read: dominant) culture, creating an atmosphere ripe for a culture clash (Strecher, 1971). The constant clash of cultures did much to wear down a police officer's "cheery disposition" (a topic about which Niederhoffer had much to say, and to which we turn momentarily). In addition to advancing the us versus them police culture, the criminal justice "system" chafed against other cultural mores close to the heart of policing. First, it engrained the need to maintain officer solidarity through secrecy, perennially referred to as the "blue code of silence" (Kappeler, Sluder, & Alpert, 1998). Now, though, the police needed to maintain professional "trade secrets" not just from the public, but from the other parts of the justice system. To wit, Van Maanen (1974) reported, "As one patrol veteran suggested: 'How the fuck can I tell anyone who ain't a cop that I lie a little in court[?]'" (p. 103). One would think that if the officer could trust *other* non-cop criminal justice actors, that he would not need to hide his perjury from the judge or prosecutor. Second, it pushed against the police culture's ethos of autonomy (Kappeler, Sluder, & Alpert, 1998). Simply stated, police had to play well with other justice agencies. But doing so, at least in the eyes of many police officers, only served to undermine the very justice which they were charged with administering.

Street Justice

The police were able to overcome this challenge to their autonomy by capitalizing on the very quality that both made their discretion necessary and unavoidable: the fact that their behavior, even their public behavior, was most often done away from supervisory eyes. The veteran officer quoted above by Van Maanen (1974) also stated that "How the fuck can I tell anyone who ain't a cop... that I made some asshole 'cause he was just all out wrong[?]" (p. 103). This behavior was described in the academic journals by Gary Sykes in a 1986 article as "street justice": "informal distributive and retributive justice in situations where individuals violated community norms and impinged on the personal and property rights of others" (p. 497). The key to street justice is the *informal* nature of it all. To borrow a cliche, police become the judge, jury, and executioner of any behavior that they deemed worthy of their attention. Such behavior may or may not be condemned by the law, as such; hence Sykes's qualification of "community norms."

Sykes noted that street justice was a natural development out of the professional model. We have already seen that while the professional model tried to limit or at least control discretion, the ABF survey revealed just how poorly it had done so. Sykes's argument in his "Street Justice: A Moral

Defense of Order Maintenance Policing" was that not only was discretionary behavior inevitable, it was, in fact, desirable. If the ABF survey and *Crime in a Free Society* represented the empirical reality of police officer discretion, Sykes's position represented the normative reality of discretion. It was not, however, without controversy. In the same issue of *Justice Quarterly*, Carl Klockar wrote a rebuttal titled "Street Justice: Some Micro-Moral Reservations: Comment on Sykes." (A bit of an irony, considering that Klockars had defended the logical extension of street justice in his article in *The Annals* in 1980 titled "The Dirty Harry Dilemma," discussed below in terms of noble cause corruption.) Klockars argued that Sykes was essentially calling for a return to the style of policing that went on prior to the professional era, similar to the arguments made by Wilson and Kelling in their famous 1982 article, "Broken Windows"—an article that was a cornerstone to Sykes's thesis. But, noted Klockars, the professional era had replaced *that* previous era for several reasons. Just because professional policing was not flawless did not mean we ought to regress, he argued, as that era, too, had its problems.

Klockars and Sykes may have disagreed on the role of order maintenance policing, but their arguments both grew out of the lack of direction that policing was experiencing at the nadir of police professionalism. Both wrote from a theoretical underpinning firmly rooted in the democratic quality of American policing, and both agreed that the professional model was inadequate and unsustainable. But the ideals of a democratic police force, perhaps first articulated the most radically by John Angell's 1971 article, "Toward an Alternative to the Classic Police Organizational Arrangements: A Democratic Model" would never fully be realized. The closest the police would ever come would be in John J. DiIulio's (1993) description of the criminal justice system as one of the co-production of justice in cooperation with citizens and the creation and funding of the federal Community Oriented Policing Services office (discussed further in chapter 9). Ultimately, Walker's (1998) assessment of the criminal justice system would prove correct: it is the nation's most *un*democratic institutions, namely the courts and the police, that would preserve and protect its democratic ideals. But neither Sykes nor Klockars would have the final say on street justice; both leading up to and certainly following their debate, scholars were describing a "new" form of police corruption that, too, was based on a morality.

Noble Cause Corruption

John Crank and Michael Caldero (2000) are the most well-known scholars associated with the idea of noble cause corruption; their work, however, is only the most recent in a long line of academic interest in the "corruption of noble cause." As far back as Ernest Hopkins (1931), interested scholars were taking note of police behavior that was motivated more by the ends than by the means to those ends. In the late 1970s and 1980s, this topic was more fully visited by William Muir (1977) and Carl Klockars (1980). And in the 21st century, I have considered a theoretical approach to understanding noble cause corruption (Cooper, 2010). Indeed, although there is little research into this topic, it has received attention from positivists, theorists, and philosophers (e.g., DeLattre, 2006) alike.

Its enduring, albeit thin, presence in policing science must be attributed, at least in part, to the fact that, unlike other forms of corruption, there is something *good* about this particular form. Crank and Caldero (2000) simply defined it as corruption "committed in the name of good ends" (p. 2). Klockars (1980) talked about what would later be labeled as noble cause corruption as the Dirty Harry Problem. According to him, the Dirty Harry Problem presented police with an insoluble moral dilemma: sometimes, the only way to achieve a good, desired (Klockars used the phrase "compelling and un-questionable"; p. 36) end when the only means available were bad, dirty, or simply immoral. Klockars, for example, gave the example of Detective Callahan torturing the serial killer Scorpio to find out where the latter had hidden a kidnapped young girl. Other examples might include planting evidence; perjury; lying to a suspect about something otherwise benign; etc.

The decades under review in this book only exasperated the need (and occasion) for the police to engage in this noble cause corruption. Discretion, the strengthening of the police culture, with its code of silence and us versus them attitude, combined with the perceived need (and perceived acceptance, in some respects) of street justice led to new forms of noble cause corruption. While noble cause corruption may, in a certain light, seem like a positive behavior, there are dangers associated with it. First is the procedural danger: if noble cause corruption led a police officer to ignore or infringe on due process, this constitutionally jeopardizes a case. Second, there is the concern, as Ivkovic (2005) pointed out, that noble cause corruption may devolve into not-so-noble corruption, as was the case with the infamous Buddy Boys of the NYPD, who went from punishing drug dealers to extorting from them. Finally, any sort of unethical behavior on the part of the police undermines the trust people have in the police, thus threatening the legitimacy of the police as an institution (Cooper & Bolen, 2013). Given the nature of the relationship between the police and the public during these three decades, the behavior defined as "noble cause corruption" could only serve to do further harm.

Occupational Anomie and the Cynicism of Police Officer

The ethos that underlines noble cause corruption was put by Crank and Caldero (2000) as "when police officers care too much" (p. 2). This value of

wanting to help people, of compassion, and of desiring to protect the innocent has been revealed in survey after survey (for the most recent study, as
well as for a review of the pertinent literature, see Cooper, White, Ward,
Saunders, & Raganella, 2014). But the very fact that something like noble
cause corruption can exist—a corruption in which the means are circumvent-
ed in the name of good ends—presupposes obstacles to the fulfillment of this
noble ethos. The structures of the professional police organization, the
"handcuffing" of the police under the "dictatorship" of the Warren Court,
and the newly systematized paradigm of the administration of justice presented the police with a number of such obstacles. While some may have responded with noble yet corrupt activity, others simply became embittered at
their job and society—and still others experienced both.

In one of the most influential policing studies of the 20th century, Arthur
Niederhoffer described this state of police officer bitterness with unadorned
blandness: cynicism. His 1969 book, *Behind the Shield*, described the ultimate source of this cynicism as an institutional state of anomie. Borrowing
not only from Durkheim, but also from contemporary anomie scholars, such
as Albert Cohen and Lloyd Ohlin, Niederhoffer explained that the social and
institutional factors, that we have been concerned with in this and previous
chapters, were insurmountable—eventually, the bad guy would go free, and
all the officer's efforts would be for nought. The result was a cynical attitude
toward their profession and toward civilians. This attitude manifested itself
in poor treatment of civilians and a relatively laissez-faire attitudes vis-a-vis
due process. The systems approach aggravated this cynicism by undoing all
the police officer's hard work. For example, by letting "scumbugs" go on
technicalities, or by engaging in ethically dubious plea bargains, the courts
created what has been described as a "revolving door of justice." Seeing this
only added to the police's feelings of bitterness, betrayal, and isolation. This,
too, would have to be changed in the decades to come.

CONCLUSIONS

Scott Decker, in his forward to Klofas, Hipple, and McGarrell's (2010) *The
New Criminal Justice*, places the President's Commission's report on par
with other watershed events in the history of criminal justice reform, such as
the 1931 Wickersham Commission report, which transformed the justice
system from a hodgepodge of agencies driven by local politics to a standardized and highly professionalized profession. He drives home the relevance of
the *Challenge of Crime in a Free Society* when he noted that "the 1967
President's Commission… played a substantial role in moving the practice of
criminal justice forward from its traditional 'practice as usual' military model
into one that had the potential for the use of data, science, and policy assess-

ment" (p. xiii). But *Crime in a Free Society*, aided by the earlier ABF survey, set the police, and, indeed, the entire justice "system," on a trajectory that reverberates today. Essentially, the value of *Challenge of Crime in a Free Society*, its flowchart, and its reimagining of the administration of justice through the lenses of the systems approach, lay in the fact that it would eventually push police away from traditional methods of law enforcement (as described in detail in chapters 2 and 4) toward a data-drive, evidenced-based approach (indeed, it would have this effect on the *entire* criminal justice system). In part, the police were always "data-driven," as witnessed by the development of the UCR and the eagerness of early 20th century police reformers to integrate mechanical and electronic technology. But, as Decker points out, in the 1960s and 1970s, the police simply lacked the technology to make data as accessible as it is today.

This is related to another effect that the systems approach had on the police that would take a few decades to fully surface: realizing that they had to work with other parts of the criminal justice system, and that what *all* the agencies in that system did impacted all the other agencies, in tandem with the new accessibility to data, facilitated the sort of interagency, crime-control collaboration we are seeing today, and as Klofas, Hipple, and McGarrell (2010) describe in detail in the first chapter of *The New Criminal Justice*. Eventually, crime control in America would leak from the hands of the police, and spread itself over the entire justice system and, to a lesser but still important extent, the public. As described in further detail in chapter 9, and laid out by Klofas and colleagues, the "new" criminal justice would be characterized by expanded legal powers, locally focused efforts, and data-based law enforcement with an emphasis on problem solving, rather than reactive policing based on calls for service. Each of these was lacking in the professional model to an appreciable degree.

This paradigmatic change from a systems approach to a collaborative data-driven approach was necessitated because of the flaws of the systems approach itself. (From the beginning, the flowchart had its detractors; for a review, see Kelling & Coles, 1998 and Walker, 2015) Specifically, the flowchart created from the systems paradigm, while exposing the inaccuracy of the professional model, was itself a largely inaccurate representation of how cases actually moved through the justice system. For one, it failed to take into account the motivation and intentions of criminal justice personnel (Klofas, Hipple, & McGarrell, 2010). But more importantly, it did not portray that *administrative nature* of the *administration of justice* (Walker, 2015).

Additionally, this research and these changes would provide police with a fourth source of discretion: *policing innovations.* This category is closely related to the organizational structure. Several police innovations over the past thirty years have required increased discretion on the part of patrol officers, including community oriented policing (COP; Trojanowicz & Bucqueroux, 1990) and problem-oriented policing (POP; Goldstein, 1979; 1990). POP, as envisioned by Goldstein (1979; 1990), has patrol officers regularly working to identify problems, creating and implementing solutions, and even evaluating the effectiveness of their solutions. This explicitly places in the hands of patrol officers a new kind of discretion that may have little to do with law enforcement, as traditionally understood. Similarly, COP properly understood encompasses a range of philosophical, strategic, tactical, and organizational changes to an agency (Cordner, 1999). It broadens the police function from law enforcement and order maintenance to include, among other things, community building and problem solving. These non-enforcement tasks, according to Cordner (1999), empower patrol officers with new discretion that, again, goes beyond the boundaries espoused by professional policing. In both cases, these innovations serve as sources of police officer discretion.

Each of these themes, among others, will be more fully explored in chapter nine. At the moment, I consider social science research conducted during these three decades, and their impact on policing, in the following chapter.

Chapter Seven

Social Science Research

This chapter discusses pivotal empirical research undertaken, especially in the 1970s, about the effectiveness of various police functions, including: the Kansas City Preventive Patrol Experiment (Kelling, et al. 1974); research on rapid response time (Pate, et al. 1976); and the effectiveness of detectives in solving crime (Greenwood & Petersilia, 1975), among others. These studies put into question the effectiveness of the professional policing model and its traditional reactive tactics, suggesting that perhaps police were not the professional crime fighters Vollmer had envisioned them to be (as discussed in chapter 2). With chapter 8, this chapter demonstrates that police were not seen as effective in fighting crime. This, along with a poor relationship with society, pushed the police into a state of transition.

Policing scholarship—both theoretical and empirical—blossomed in the 1960s and 70s at the university level like never before. For example, prior to the publication of *Challenge of Crime in a Free Society* in 1967, there were 12 books published on the police. Since the President's Commission's published report, there have been about 3000 books. Similarly, prior to 1967, there were about 70 university dissertations on the police (including Westley's dissertation, completed in 1951, that would have to wait until 1970 to see publication but would be hugely influential once in print), compared to over 1200 successfully defended dissertations after that "time stamp" (National Research Council [NRC], 2004). The impact was not limited to the police:

> The cascade of peer-reviewed research on the police since 1967 has been part of the development of criminal justice studies generally. Of the 12 most highly regarded journals in criminology and police studies published today, only 3 existed before 1967. Altogether, these journals have published over 6,900 articles dealing with the police and law enforcement, the larger part after 1967.

Sociological Abstract, which covers 2,500 journals and periodicals, lists 6,929
citations to material published between 1963 and 2001. (NRC, 2004, p. 21)

The Academy of Criminal Justice Sciences has long housed a Policing Section, which is responsible for the newsletter *Police Forum* and, in partnership with the Police Executive Research Forum (PERF), the refereed journal *Police Quarterly*. And since 2014, the American Society of Criminology has housed its own Division on Policing (an irony considering that the ASC's founding can be traced back to August Vollmer and a number of early 20th century policing scholars, instructors, and practitioners; cf. Morris, 1975). Both subunits of these national organizations represent the degree to which policing scholarship has come, and where it is going.

At least two events conspired in the 1960s and 1970s to bring about the enormous increase in policing research: the rising crime rate (covered in the next chapter) and race riots (covered in preceding chapters, especially four) and the creation of the federal Law Enforcement Assistance Administration office (LEAA) and its child, the Law Enforcement Education Program (LEEP). The rising crime rate, in tandem with the race riots, garnered intense national attention, which translated into political attention, resulting in Johnson's 1965 call for a "war on crime" (with devastating results that reverberate today; cf. Walker, 2015: "Waging 'War' Is The Wrong Way to Fight Crime," p. 17). Scholars seemed no less aware of the political and public news than lay persons, and were quick to take advantage of this new (and relatively deserved) media craze. They were aided by the federal government, both in its publication of *Challenge of Crime in a Free Society* and in founding LEAA, which provided a number of monies for policing research. Included in these monies were resources for universities to create departments of criminal justice through the LEAP. Although these academic departments began as "cop-shops," with classes in traffic direction and handcuffing, most of these programs would evolve into the social science departments that dot the American university landscape of today. But at their beginnings, the new college departments needed faculty, and much of that faculty would engage in research. And so the interest in policing scholarship was nurtured.

It was not only universities that engaged in policing research: private foundations also played an integral part in this explosive research agenda. Both PERF and the Police Foundation (PF) were founded in the 1970s—PERF in 1976 (incorporated in 1981—see their website for details), and PF in 1970 with funding from the Ford Foundation. PF was especially seminal in these early years if for no other reason than it was involved in the execution of what remains one of the most famous, influential, and discussed studies in policing scholarship history, the Kansas City Preventive Patrol experiment (which, along with Martinson's comment on "nothing works," discussed in chapter 5, also remains one of the most misunderstood and misapplied studies in the canon of criminology). Before discussing this (and other policing studies), I first consider four studies that resulted in book-length publications that preceded much of this research. Additionally, they provided (and to a great degree yet provide) the theoretical underpinnings for the policing experiments and studies that would follow.

PRECURSORS

Our "time stamp," as indicated above, is the 1967 publication of *Challenge of Crime in a Free Society*, because it was this event that, more than the others, gave justification and provided the Kuhnian interest necessary for policing research to take off the way that it did. Among the four books reviewed below, the ABF's survey covered in the previous chapter also deserves a place. As will become readily apparently, an overwhelming amount of policing research has been—and remains—concerned not only with *what* police do, but *why* they do it. In other words, policing scholarship by and large is focused on the topic of *police discretion*. Similarly, and as already discussed both above and in previous chapters, the President's Commission's *Challenge of Crime in a Free Society* was itself an exhaustive study, and so it, too, can rightly be considered a precursor to the studies with which the rest of this chapter is concerned. For now, we consider four seminal books: William Westley's 1951 dissertation which was later published in book form in 1970 under the title *Violence and the Police: A Sociological Study of Law, Custom and Morality*; Jerome Skolnick's (1966) *Justice without Trial*; Jonathan Rubinstein's (1973) *City Police*; and James Q. Wilson's (1968) *Varieties of Police Behavior*.

Violence and the Police

Westley's doctoral work went largely ignored after its completion (Walker, 1998), and continued to be ignored even after it was published as a research article in the prestigious *American Journal of Sociology* (*AJS*) in 1953. That his study of the police in Gary, Indiana, was ignored until the 1970s is not an indictment of its methodological rigour or scientific value; indeed, Westley's is only one of about a dozen articles on policing that *AJS* has *ever* published (see NRC, 2004, p. 22 for details on the small amount of policing articles published in flagship sociology journals over the last fifty years). Rather, it was largely due to *timing*. Prior to 1967, according to a search on Google Scholar, Westley's *AJS* article was cited about twenty times, compared to ninety-nine times during the same number of years after 1967. It was cited a total 275 times since 1967, or on average six times per year, as opposed to about one and a half times per year up to 1967. Fortunately, Westley had the awareness to realize that his study was still of value twenty years later, and so he published his dissertation in book form in 1970 when the winds of policing research were changing. His text, *Violence and the Police*, has been cited over 400 times since its publication.

In Westley's work with the police of Gary, he uncovered a number of occupational patterns that students and scholars of policing today take for granted. For example, he found that socialization into what Skolnick would later call the police working personality was exceptionally strong, and was reinforced early and often. Additionally, Westley noted that police would brook absolutely no disrespect, and refused to back down from any sign of challenge to their authority. This created tension between the police and society—especially among minorities, but also among the dominant class and race. So it was no surprise that Westley also observed that police felt that the public did not support their crime fighting efforts, as almost all of their interactions with the public were confrontational. This only reinforced a strong in-group solidarity that I have talked about throughout my book as an *us versus them* attitude. Additionally, this solidarity was supported by the bulwark of what Westley and others would describe as a wall or code of silence.

Justice without Trial

Jerome Skolnick's (1966) work with "Westville" and its police department would underscore and build upon a number of the findings first uncovered by Westley. Indeed, Skolnick cited Westley over a dozen times in *Justice without Trial*, often quoting him directly. Of Westley, Skolnick wrote: "[he] was the first to raise such questions about the police, when he inquired into the conditions under which police are violent. Whatever merit this analysis has, it owes much to his prior insights, as all subsequent sociological studies of the police must" (p. 274). Much of what Westley talked about can be seen in Skolnick's characterization of the *police working personality*. This "working personality" was, according to Skolnick (1966), wrapped up in those questions that he attributes ultimately to Westley: "What are the conditions under which police, as authorities, may be threatened" (p. 41). Skolnick would conclude that the police working personality—those characteristics that defined how the police officer went about doing his job—was predicated on two foundations: authority and perceived danger.

The police were endowed with the state sanctioned authority to enforce laws and, to a large extent, morality. But this authority was exercised in an environment where people were personally and willfully *breaking* those laws and bending morality, creating a situation that inheres danger for those charged with enforcing the laws of the land. The net result was not only a strong group solidarity, but what might be described as an introverted group solidarity. By "introverted," I mean the habit of police to socialize only with other police. This was necessitated because, as Skolnick would write, "the character of the police work makes the police officer less desirable as a friend since norms of friendship implicate others in the police officer's work" (p. 41). What he meant by this sentence was that *everyone* breaks the law and public morality at some point. Such behavior triggers the "official" behavior on the part of the police. But *friends* do not get other friends in trouble. Thus, "normal" friendship must be avoided by the police. This could only serve to further isolate them from the public. Further, this knowledge that everyone can commit a crime, coupled with the ever present danger described by Skolnick as the "symbolic assailant" would imbue the police with a suspicious outlook on life bordering on the paranoid.

The concept of the "symbolic assailant" was extremely important to Skolnick's development of the police working personality. The symbolic assailant can be understood as a hypothesized amalgam of all the "dirt bags" with whom the police have ever interacted. It is a collective hypothetical, experientially shared between police officers in a process of socialization. The basic idea can be described thusly: people who are dangerous can be identified by certain characteristics that separate them from non-dangerous people. Importantly, these identifiers are *not* criminal. Thus characteristics such as dress, race, class, language, and demeanor came to signify people who cannot be trusted, and must be controlled. At this point in the current book, the reader should not be surprised that white and middle class Americans did *not* fit the symbolic assailant mold. Thus Skolnick, too, would anticipate the empirical support of the poor relations between police and minorities.

Skolnick added (at least) one more insight into our understanding of the police that still resonates today. He noted that the behavior of the police was largely oriented toward *production*. For Skolnick, *production* was understood as the output of a department's goals, and the tasks associated with those goals. The real implications of this insight would not truly be understood until James Fyfe would investigate police officer "fleeing felon" shootings in the 1980s (a study discussed below). But this idea that the *work* of the police was motivated by goals and tasks meant that it was *not* reliant, necessarily, on *fighting crime*. It was only reliant on fighting crime insofar as it composed some goal or goals of the police. Further, it would only relate to *fighting crime* if those goals were rationally connected to their *tasks*. As Jonathan Rubinstein would discover, this was rarely the case.

City Police

In my own experience, nothing is more foundational to understanding how police agencies behave than the seminal work of Jonathan Rubinstein. Rubinstein, a journalist, joined the Philadelphia police as a patrol officer. He wrote *City Police* (1973), which is based on his experiences and observations. Just as Westley, Skolnick, and, originally, the ABF observed, the police were not necessarily enforcing the law as it was prescribed on the books. Rather, Rubinstein wrote that their behavior was determined by the interaction of two particular concerns: control over their *territory*, and what he labeled as the production of *activity*. In a theme that would later be developed further by David Klinger (1997), Robert Kane (2002), and myself (Cooper, 2014), Rubinstein observed that police behavior was relegated within the territory for which they were responsible. Indeed, when police look at a city, they don't see a collection of streets and blocks: they see "a mosaic of linked districts [i.e., precincts]" (p. 26). Van Maanen (1974) would soon corroborate this observation in his own work, noting that "patrolmen are tied inextricably" (p. 113) to these areal units. This territoriality is perhaps best demonstrated by something a police officer once said to me while I was on a ride along: "You know a place is bad if the police have a name for it."

Territory matters to the police because they are assigned to patrol and protect a specific areal unit—ultimately the precinct, but day-to-day the beat. The neighborhoods and communities that make up that areal unit—which may or may not coincide with the police officer's territorial boundaries—are filtered differently for the officer than for the civilian. Not only is there a difference in geographical outlook but there is a difference in priority. While the civilian may be concerned with crime generally—or, more likely, with disorder—the police officer, as Rubinstein (1973) uncovered, is concerned with something subtly different: activity. In *City Police*, he described activity in the following terms:

> [t]he worth of a man to his platoon does not depend on his success in preventing crimes, arresting suspected felons, or even giving service without complaint or injury… "Activity" is the internal product of police work. It is the statistical measure which the sergeant uses to judge the productivity of his men…Arrest activity is computed from what the patrolman "puts on the books" and not by the disposition of his cases in court. Since activity is a measure of his work, his sergeant has no interest in what eventually happens to the cases. (pp. 44–45)

What Rubinstein is saying here is that a) police behavior is not actually geared toward crime prevention, and b) is not concerned with citizen satisfaction. These two elements obviously would play an important role in *why* the race riots occurred—and, as will be revealed in chapter 9, were taken seriously in all following attempts at police reform.

In addition, Rubinstein is pointing out that c) police behavior is largely dictated by *numbers* (something Skolnick and Fyfe in their 1993 book *Above the Law* would quote one officer as lovingly referring to as the "fucking numbers game")—specifically, the *production of numbers*. There is a difference between the *subtraction* of numbers that one would expect from a visible deterrent force, as hoped for by Sir Robert Peel, and the *production* of numbers supported by the Uniform Crime Reports and the "putting on the books" of activity. That is, if you deter something, it's not there, you're not measuring what you're *doing*, and so the fear is that you appear to be doing *nothing*. "Activity," on the other hand, shows that you are doing *something*—and so it (whatever *it* is), and not deterrence, becomes the primary motivating force behind your behavior.

Importantly, all this "activity" takes place *within* that officer's *territory*, and so it is that territory with which they are most concerned. Part of the genius of Rubinstein's work is the realization that these territories are political. In truth, this was something Weber wrote about decades before when he defined a nation state as a territory belonging to a social aggregate which had a vested interest in maintaining and protecting its borders, both from threats within and without (cf. Weber, 2004). In the United States, the police are charged with keeping the peace *within* those borders. They do so within a territorial framework, as described above. But the police officer's territory is not an emergent, meso-level phenomenon, as one would describe a community or neighborhood. Rather, they are wholly politically constructed. Because they are politically constructed, the police are themselves strongly influenced by politics—something that James Q. Wilson outlined in his policing classic, *Varieties of Police Behavior*.

Varieties of Police Behavior

While a good number of readers will be familiar with the works of Westley, Rubinstein, and Skolnick, it is almost certain that nearly all will at least be aware of James Q. Wilson's pioneering policing study (if not, they are most definitely aware of his 1982 article with George Kelling, "Broken Windows"). Published in 1968 as *Varieties of Police Behavior*, Wilson articulated the orientations that eight police departments took toward the administration of justice. Of course, Wilson, too, found that the administration of justice was understood in very broad brushstrokes by police. He distilled what the police dealt with into two categories: law enforcement and order maintenance. He noted, as others have before and since, that whereas the public (and to a large extent the police themselves) perceived that the bulk of police work was spent in enforcing the law, in reality it was in order maintenance. *How* the police went about navigating order maintenance determined, for Wilson, their orientation toward the administration of justice.

Wilson described three such orientations: watchman, service, and legalistic. *Watchman* agencies have the greatest latitude in how they deal with the maintenance of order, whereas *legalistic* arguably have the least latitude. In the former, officers are given, basically, complete agency to handle order maintenance issues however they would prefer. In the latter, they are not only given strict guidelines, but those guidelines can best be described as the *letter of the law*: whatever the books say is disorder, and however the books direct officers to deal with such disorder, then that's what and how they should do it. These orientations are contrasted to the third, the *service* style. Service style agencies do not give their officers much latitude in terms of how order is maintained, or which disorder offenses to focus on, but they are not as "by-the-book" as legalistic agencies. Rather, the *what* and *how* of their order maintenance activities is determined by the community that they service. This requires a community that is homogeneous, in large part because many times the community prefers *informal* means of handling disorder offenses, which assumes a certain level of consensus on what is acceptable on the part of the police.

As useful as this typology is, Wilson's real insight concerned the *source* of such different orientations. Wilson argued that such variety in behavior among police agencies existed because the political structures of American municipalities also varied. And it was these different political structures which, although to a large degree were previously misunderstood only in terms of what has been labeled the "political era of policing" (see chapter 2), explained the distinct orientations of police departments vis-a-vis order maintenance. Wilson explained this political effect as being exerted indirectly *through* the agency's organizational culture: the political structure influences the organizational culture which in turn impacts officer decision making (or lack thereof) during the order maintenance process. Wilson's insight added yet another layer to understanding the discretionary behavior of the police, and provided novel theoretical questions that previously had not crossed the minds of social scientists. Research has both confirmed and questioned Wilson's typology and its relationship to municipal politics (for an overview, see Zhao & Hassell, 2005), but its impact and contribution to the developing canon of policing research in the social sciences is beyond dispute (in fact, Google scholar lists over two thousand citations for *Varieties of Police Behavior* across its editions).

POLICING RESEARCH IN THE 1960S AND 1970S: A SURVEY

The collective outcome of these books, in tandem with the ABS survey and *Challenge of Crime in a Free Society*, was a frank and sudden (as far as that word applies to the protracted nature of academe) burst of empirical research. Criminology and criminal justice were coming into their own as academic disciplines, slowly divorcing themselves from their earlier parents, such as sociology, psychology, economics, philosophy, and political science. As already indicated above, refereed journals focusing solely on criminology were becoming more common, and it was becoming standard for state schools, and later private schools, to house departments and programs of criminology and/or criminal justice. This, along with the founding of the National Institute of Justice under the 1968 Omnibus Crime Control and Safety Act, created an environment that encouraged and nourished this new line of research—and in most cases *supported* it via federal research grants.

The new research, while building on its predecessors, differed markedly in terms of content. Stemming from the "discovery" of police discretion, these earlier books were largely focused on what police *did* and *why*. Initial studies, such as some of those I reviewed above, were largely ethnographic and qualitative in nature, using variations of the observer-as-participant model. Sometimes this meant extensive interviewing and ride-alongs; other times, as with Rubinstein (1973), it meant actually joining a police force. Rubinstein was a journalist, and his approach to studying the police reflects this. Early on, but more and more commonly after Rubinstein, policing research would become more systematized, as with Wilson's (1968) *Varieties of Police Behavior*.

This has never been a methodology left to the wayside of policing research; however, the studies that followed the works of Rubinstein, Wilson, Westley, and Skolnick began to shift their focus to the area of crime control (NRC, 2004); in other words, the question was no longer simply *what were the police doing,* but *were the police effective?* Although it's a qualified *no,* the answer to which the corpus of this research came was nevertheless *no, police were* not *effective in controlling or fighting crime.* Appropriately, the methods changed to meet the new questions, as surveys became more common. Eventually, policing research would evolve into what we now call *evaluation research* (NRC, 2004). Evaluation research are studies undertaken to understand whether a particular criminal justice practice or policy had its intended outcome—and *why* (Cooper & Worrall, 2012). It was *this* body of research that was most devastating for the police. I begin my brief survey of this research with what must be considered the most influential study of the effectiveness of police behavior: the Kansas City Preventive Patrol Experiment.

Kansas City Preventive Patrol Experiment

The Kansas City Preventive Patrol Experiment (hereafter KCPPE), at its core, had a very simple goal: to scientifically test the founding proposition of the police, namely, their ability to deter crime through a visible presence. To the uninitiated the need to even test such a proposition may seem unnecessary because of the intuitive appeal of visible deterrence. And indeed, many people—police, scholars, and laypersons alike—remain convinced that the deterrence of crime by the justice system, including the police, is a valid assumption. This book is not the venue to argue for or against the merits of deterrence theory; it suffices to simply say that the "jury is still out" on just how adequate of a job deterrence theory does in predicting crime, and consequently how effectively criminal justice policies based on the theory of deterrence perform (for an overview, see Cullen, Wright, & Blevins, 2009, especially chapter 13 by Pratt et al., "The Empirical Status of Deterrence Theory: A Meta-Analysis"). But it is important to point out that the KCPPE represented the *first effort to put this proposition to the test after over 150 years of being put into practice.* The idea that the utility of the police lay in their ability to deter crime through their presence was articulated clearly by Sir Robert Peel in his 1829 legislation that gave birth to modern policing, which was transported, in principle if not in operation, by American police (see chapter 2). But its origins in criminal justice extend back to at least Jeremy Bentham in his *An Introduction to the Principles of Morals and Legislations* published in 1789, and Cesare Beccaria's 1764 *On Crimes and Punishment.*

That aspect alone makes the KCPPE novel and important. But the manner in which it came about renders it doubly so: although the experiment was completed in cooperation with PF, it was partly the brain-child of the revolutionary chief of police of Kansas City, Clarence Kelley. Samuel Walker and Charles Katz (2011), in their popular introductory policing textbook, *The Police in America*, describe Kelley's decision to house an experiment on preventive patrol a "gamble" because of the very real possibility that it may have been found that patrol did *nothing* in terms of crime deterrence. If that was the case, what sort of backlash would Kelley—and other police departments—face? It ended up being a wise course of action for Kelley, as his bold move to engage in social science research resonated with the times, and he was appointed as director of the FBI before the experiment's completion.

The methodology of the KCPPE is well known to any criminology or criminal justice student who has taken a class on research methodology—it is the poster child for both the advantages and challenges of running experiments "outside the lab." The study was designed to test the effects of visible deterrence *through* random car patrol. The Kansas City Police Department's South Patrol District was divided into three groups of beats: proactive, reactive, and control. Proactive groups essentially received double the amount of patrol, compared to control groups which received the normal amount of patrol, and reactive beats which had no random patrol. Both criminal activity and citizen perceptions were observed, via agency records and survey data. The net effect of random patrol in Kansas City was null: neither crime nor the perception of crime was in any way impacted by patrol. The KCPPE was administered in 1972–1973, and was later confirmed in 1978–89 through the Newark Foot Patrol experiment (although this latter experiment also found that random foot patrol *did* reduce citizen fear of crime and improved attitudes of citizens toward police).

Despite the intuitive appeal of deterrence, it was not wholly supported by the KCPPE. Why was this? In part, it has to do with the methodology of the KCPPE, and in part with the nature of policing. It was flawed insofar as it was unlikely that citizens even noticed the change in patrol saturation. For example, even the reactive beats would receive "patrol" as cars traveled to calls for service, either within the reactive beat or on the way to other beats. Additionally, Sherman and Weisburd (1995) pointed out that police patrol is spread rather thin, which limits the extent to which it can actually *be* a visible presence. The KCPPE did have an impact on police practice and research, however, leading to a number of patrol innovations, such as directed patrol, and theoretical concepts, such as residual deterrence, that would be found effective by later research (some of which is discussed below). More than this, perhaps, is the precedent that the KCPPE created for the importance *and* feasibility of deliberate policing research. In this sense, then, the KCPPE continues to resonate today in policing scholarship—including in the pages of this book.

Research on Patrol

Research during this time period was done on pretty much everything about patrol: the culture, rapport with the public, effectiveness, etc. Ultimately, the research on patrol can be boiled down to *discretion*: what were police doing, why, and in what way did it matter? One of the most detailed studies about police discretion was Michael Brown's *Working the Street: Police Discretion and the Dilemmas of Reform*. Although Brown's research was first published in 1981, it reflects research he conducted during the 1970s in three southern California cities. In his work, he suggests that how police use their discretion can be explained by an appeal to two variables, what he calls an officer's *aggressiveness* and *selectivity*. By aggressiveness, Brown meant the extent to which an officer looks for law enforcement opportunities, and by selectivity he meant the degree to which an officer was only concerned with serious crimes. From these two variables, Brown defined four officers, characterized by the manner in which they deployed their discretion.

1. *clean-beat crime fighters* are high in aggressiveness, but low in selectivity, and so rigorously enforce all laws in almost all possible situations
2. *old-style crime fighters* are high in both aggressiveness and selectivity, choosing to focus on only the most serious crimes, and actively seeking them out
3. *service-style officers* are high in selectivity, choosing to focus on serious crimes, but low in aggressiveness, and so do not actively seek out the opportunity to enforce even serious crimes

4. *professional-style officers* are low on both aggressiveness and selectivity, tending to focus on order maintenance only when the situation presents itself

Brown did not suggest that an officer was predisposed to use their discretion according to this typology; rather, he pointed out that how an officer used discretion was a complex interaction of the individual officer, the neighborhood in which he worked, his organizational culture, as well as the specific situation in which the officer might find himself.

Brown's work not only provided a useful heuristic for talking about how (and why) officers use discretion, but also supported findings from previous research that such discretion is employed differentially from situation to situation. Albert Reiss (1968) found, for example, that blacks were much more likely to be shot by the police than whites, a finding that Fyfe would replicate later in the 1980s (discussed more fully below). It is not surprising that so much of policing research in the 1960s and 70s would be dominated by issues of race and gender, given the *zeitgeist* of the times. For example, the "Police Services Study" of 1977, which resulted in at least two publications, including Visher (1983) and Smith, Visher, & Davidson (1984). The latter publication looked at both suspect-driven bias and victim-driven bias among officers—in other words, did the race of the suspect or the victim impact the officer's discretion? They found that while the race of the suspect did not seem to matter in their sample (which included the cities of St. Louis, Rochester, and St. Petersburg), the race of the *victim* did, insofar as white victims received more attention than their minority counterparts.

The effectiveness (or, rather, the effect) of response time also came under scrutiny during this time period. It was repeatedly found that faster response time had no effect on arrests. Research found, however, that response time *did* matter in terms of how the public *felt* toward the police. For example, Furstenburg and Wellford (1973) found that public satisfaction in the police began to drop after fifteen minutes of wait time. These two findings would result in *differential response time,* where police treat certain calls for service differently in terms of how quickly they arrive at these calls. The citizens are typically informed of how long of a wait they would have to have. This strategy seemed to satisfy those who placed calls for service without making crime rates rise (Cahn & Tien, 1981).

Finally, several studies, in the spirit of the KCPPE, evaluated various police programs. Many of these would be conducted later in the 1980s, such as PF's collaborative study with the Minneapolis Police Department on police response to domestic violence calls for service. Collectively, they demonstrated not just an evolving interest in policing research, but an evolution of policing research methodology. A world of methodological difference exists between the New York Police Department's 1950s "experiment" called Operation 25 and the KCPPE, for example. Operation 25, which considered increasing patrol up to three times in the 25th Precinct, claimed to reduce muggings and auto theft. But unlike the KCPPE, it was not conducted independently, nor did it take into account potential displacement effects caused by saturation patrol. In short, it left much to be desired. Although the KCPPE is often held up as the poster child of why experiments are so difficult in criminology, for its time it was novel and sophisticated. And if we police scholars are to be honest with ourselves, it *remains* one of the most sophisticated designs in the corpus of our literature, which is inundated with cross-sectional designs and one-shot case studies.

Research on Detectives

Although the bulk of policing research being done during this time period—as well as now—focused on patrol officers, scholars also spent time studying detectives and investigative work. This pattern, too, built off that set forth by the President's Commission on Law Enforcement and the Administration of Justice, this time in their publication *Task Force Report: Science and Technology*, published in 1967. Among the myriad subjects that the President's Commission explored, how effective police detectives were in solving cases was at the forefront. By and large, they found that detective work, as traditionally conceived, simply did not matter—instead, suspect identification from the victim was the key. For example, in 1,905 cases examined from the Los Angeles Police Department, findings showed 86 percent of the 349 cases where the victim *could identify* the suspect were cleared, compared to 12 percent of the remaining 1,556 cases for which detectives had no suspect identification. For the LAPD, at least, detectives spent four hours on most cases—the bulk of which was in doing paperwork.

The RAND Corporation (Greenwood & Petersilia, 1975), using monies from the LEAA, found very similar results in their own study of American police detectives, but at a national level. Greenwood and Petersilia closely observed twenty-five police agencies across two years, and surveyed an additional 156 police agencies, in terms of detective work. They found that "successful" detective work hinged on victims being able to provide useful and identifying information to the police—often times to the patrol officer rather than the assigned detective. Indeed, they found that 75 percent of the time the suspect was identified upon report of the crime. Detectives, it seemed, spent most of their time managing paperwork and placating victims. Although some later research would suggest that while all this was true, police detectives *did* contribute to the practice of interrogating suspects (William & Snortom, 1984)—but even then, most suspects tended to confess. So detectives, too, were told that their job didn't matter. As such, it too would come under new reform efforts in the late 20th and early 21st centuries, that I will discuss in chapter 9.

CONCLUSIONS

This research revolution came on the heels of the Warren Court's due process revolution, and together they had a devastating effect on the relationship between the police and the public. As Walker (1998) understatedly writes, it "demolished many widely held assumptions" (p. 206) about how the police worked. And, along with Martinson's dictum that nothing worked in correctional rehabilitation, the research on the police collectively muted any hopes of reform: "It became increasingly clear, for example, that quick improvements in policing were not possible" (Walker, 1998, p. 208). What's more, the research interacted with the publicity the police were receiving regarding race riots and racial tensions: study after study revealed that not only did police have strained relations with the public, especially minority communities, but that they also treated minorities differently.

All was not so grim, however. Bayley and Mendelsohn (1969), for example, discovered early on that, while the police as a group may treat minorities differently, individual cops themselves were no less racist than average people. Indeed, they found that the police were, in general, quite average in temperament and ideology. And however the public may *feel* about the police they still relied on the police to solve all sorts of problems, from maintaining social boundaries, to relieving situations that were simply unpleasant, to say nothing of obtaining emergency services (Morrison & Meyer, 1974). More than anything, the corpus of research that came out of this time period revealed just how complex police behavior was, both to describe and explain it in any standardized way.

Once the ball was rolling, policing studies became more popular. Policing research in the 1980s (and beyond) continued to build on the theoretical questions that their predecessors had presented. PF, for example, would later collaborate with the Minneapolis Police Department in an experimental evaluation of the ways to handle domestic violence calls for service. This study occurred in the 1980s, but like its predecessor, the KCPPE, it strived for methodological rigour and practical application. And like its predecessor, it would send a shockwave across American policing—which, in a demonstration of just how important research had become to policing in the United States by then, would be stunted by a series of studies funded by the federal government to see if they could replicate the Minneapolis study's findings (ultimately, they could not).

With all of this research, the question still loomed, *could the police meaningfully change?* Research, too, was integral in providing a resounding *yes* to this question. James Fyfe (1988), for example, in the 1980s demonstrated that departmental policy *could* influence police discretion. In this case, departmental policy reduced the disparity between black versus white suspects who were shot by the police. Such research would set the stage for the 1990s and the 21st century, where meaningful reform *would* take place, but accompanied by social science in a way that it never had been before.

This was only part of the picture leading to reform. Before science would have its day in policing, two more events would be necessary, on a national scale: regular corruption among police *departments and units*—as opposed to among police *officers*—and a rising crime rate that, for the first time since the end of World War II, was increasing at a rate that could not be explained with an appeal to population inflation.

Chapter Eight

A Rising Crime Rate and Police Corruption

Prior to the 1960s, crime in the United States had been increasing concomitantly with population and immigration, with a few bumps here and there, particularly during wartime and recession. This trend ended in the 1960s, and only became worse in the 1970s, as the nation saw an enormous uptick in crime across the board that could not be explained by population growth alone. It would not be until the mid-1990s that crime rates would fall to anywhere near the pre-1960s levels. As with the events described in chapter 7, the increasing crime rate called into question the effectiveness of traditional policing tactics and strategies. In addition, the media, political, and research scrutiny exerted on the police brought systemic corruption to the attention of the nation. This was more than a "some cops are just bad apples" sort of corruption; rather, the research uncovered the sort of endemic corruption that minorities had protested against throughout the long, hot summers. Something needed to change.

Of course, not all—or even most—police departments had problems with corruption. Even large police departments were, if not wholly, at least mostly incorrupt. But such realities, in the context of the 1960s and 1970s that has been portrayed in the foregoing pages, hardly mattered when compared to the *perception* of such realities. As Kappeler, Sluder, and Alpert (1998) argue in their book on police deviance, although public perception about the police *in general* is positive, the very appearance or perception of corruption can be damaging. They further point out that corruption had continuously haunted the American police since their establishment in the early and mid nineteenth century. The corrupt relationship between the police and politics was the primary reason for law enforcement reform at the turn of the century, even though the professional-reform model was supposed to have fixed all that.

By the 1950s, it was becoming evident that it had not. Indeed, it was the Kefauver Committee (1950–1951; dealing with interstate commerce, organized crime, and police collusion) that brought police corruption to the public's attention. Things only became worse in the 1960s as corruption both preceded and endured throughout the long hot summers of race riots. In fact, it was often the corruption (or at least the misconduct) of the police that sparked many of these riots. The public and political concern over systemic police corruption would be immortalized in the movie *Serpico*, which detailed the experience of NYPD whistleblower Frank Serpico. His experience, among others, would lead up to the important Knapp Commission, which is covered later in this chapter.

The public concern over police corruption was also reflected in the burgeoning policing scholarship at the university level. This scholarship was not only part of the movement toward policing studies previously discussed in this book, but was also caught up in the systems model. For example, Lawrence Sherman in *Police Corruption* (1974—a book largely funded by the Ford Foundation) wrote that "the problem of police corruption is merely a slice of the larger problem of official corruption in American society" (p. vii). It is important to point out that Sherman was writing with the backdrop of the Watergate scandal; thus he began the preface with "The Watergate affair, though it removed police corruption from the center stage of media attention, has amply demonstrated the pervasiveness of government misconduct at every level of government" (p. vii). Be this as it may, Sherman was most certainly *not* giving police any sort of pass. On the contrary, he quickly noted that the police, while part of that same generalized government corruption, were *more* important than those involved even in Watergate:

> The policeman is *more* powerful than the President. Only the policeman has the power to deprive an American of his liberty, and only the policeman defines, on a daily basis, the law of the land. That policemen themselves are often criminals, then, may be the gravest concern for a "rule of law, not of men." Police have often complained, and quite rightly, that they have been singled out unfairly from other branches of a generally corrupt system of criminal justice...yet, again, it is the police who control the intake of the criminal justice system, which in fact makes them more important, though no more blameworthy, than the other branches of the system.

That Sherman's book was funded by the Ford Foundation is evidence enough to demonstrate how important policing research was becoming to both the public and the political power players in the United States during the 1960s and 1970s. Sherman himself argues that the very purpose of his book was, in part, to inform policy and reform efforts. Similarly, Chambliss (1971), writing three years earlier, essentially argued that while the previous scholarly efforts at police research were useful, they were ultimately exercises in journalism, and now that social scientists were invoking the scientific method in all its epistemological glory, we could expect to see real change in policing. There is some element of truth to that observation, even if it is a bit overstated—and would take a few more decades to actually see any sort of fruition. This discussion is taken up again in chapter 9. What is important to note here is that scholars believed that their efforts were important to the very practice of the police, and that government and private foundations agreed.

Given the newly intense interest in the police and deviance, in general, it is not surprising that scholars, police, and politicians were keeping a close eye on what was going on with crime. Even before the long hot summers, it was apparent that the crime rate was no longer stable and was, in fact, going up at an unexpected rate. This pattern, too, would force the public to turn a critical eye toward police behavior, policy, and practice, especially in terms of their actual effect as "crime fighters". It is to this that we turn first, concluding with a deeper discussion about how corruption was perceived and "handled" throughout the time period this book covers. Although the topics of *corruption* and the *crime rate* may seem disparate, they in fact go hand-in-hand: both led to the realization among the public and politicians that the police were neither doing what they ought to do nor achieving what they ought to do. They were both informed by and informed a growing policing research agenda within the academy that corruption was believed to have led to the increase in crime, at least in part and certainly in regard to the race riots.

THE GREAT AMERICAN CRIME SURGE

Despite the concern over crime in the United States, and without minimizing its importance, it is nevertheless accurate to point out that violent crime in the United States is, and essentially always has been, a statistically rare occurrence. Although the United States may virtually lead the developed world in crime rates, arrest rates, prison rates, and execution rates compared to other areas of the world, and other periods in world history, the United States is, overall, a very low crime nation. Even the most crime-ridden neighborhood will usually pale in comparison to other more violent nations. There are times and places where crime is an acute problem; but as a chronic issue, even in the 1980s, crime has never properly been a problem for the United States. What this means, practically speaking, is that when crime does increase, it is felt more intensely than its actual magnitude might merit. This has an enormous amount to do with both the media and politicians—both of which are wrapped up in the market-economy of American capitalism, for which crime provides an especially lucrative source of revenue. It is perhaps no surprise, then, that the crime rate would have such an impact on the lives of Americans and the police as it began to rise in the 1960s.

Samuel Walker (2011), writing with over fifty years of insight, described this impact in these dire terms: "Since the crime rates began to soar around 1963, crime has ripped the social fabric of American society and has been a major issue in American politics" (p.3). Readers may miss it at first, but the most important part of Walker's description is that he does not use the term "crime *rate*"; rather, he uses the plural, "crime rates." Although there is no consensus among criminologists about what crime is, exactly (which is a bit ironic considering that contemporary criminology has a heavy functionalist bent), their disunity demonstrates Walker's underlying reason for employing the plural "rates": crime varies according not only to the presence and absence of criminogenic covariates, but according to the type of crime. To oversimplify an incredibly complex etiological discussion, that which causes violent crime does not also cause property crime, in a one to one comparison. It is appropriate, therefore, for Walker to talk about the increase in crime *rates* as shorthand for saying, *crime across the board was increasing at a rate that caught everyone off guard.* Individual crime rates tend to fluctuate around a three year cycle (it is for this reason why sophisticated analysts use the mean crime rate of three years rather than that of a single year). The fact that virtually *all* crime rates were increasing throughout the 1960s and 1970s (and 1980s and the first part of the 1990s) alone supports Walker's contention that it "ripped the social fabric of American society." In addition, it allows us to talk about an increase in the *national aggregate crime rate* with some sense that the national increase largely reflected the increases in its constituent crime rates.

The rise in crime rates was identifiable across all crime categories, including what are considered violent crimes (Blumstein & Wallman, 2006). Thus the murder rate increased by at least a factor of two (Walker, 2011). Zimring (2008) discusses murder rates since the 1960s as being divided by the year 1975. He points out that from 1964 to 1975, the homicide rate essentially doubled; from 1975 to about 1993, it continued to increase even more than that (not dropping until the mid-1990s, with the earliest signs of a crime drop showing up in 1991). Blumstein and Wallman (2006) count the figures at about five homicides per 100,000 persons, prior to sixty-five, with a steady increase thereafter, ranging from eight to ten homicides per 100,000 persons after 1970, for more than twenty years. Homicide rates (and the crime rate more generally) did not return to their pre-1965 levels until 1999. Aggravated assault also increased during this time period—by as much as 134 percent. This number, though, is most likely a woeful underestimate. Blumstein (2006) points out this estimation error and its reasoning; it is based on police reports which rely on calls for service or that an officer actually witnessed an aggravated assault—a relatively rare occurrence. As a general rule, victimization surveys showed the same pattern of aggravated assault increase. They disagreed on the magnitude, exhibiting a much higher crime rate than police activity might have suggested (Lynch & Addington, 2006).

The etiology of this rise in crime is just as mysterious as its precipitous fall in the 1990s. To a large degree, it was pushed by demographics. Walker (2011), for example, suggests that at least half of the increase was due to baby boomers coming of age. In 1965, we would have seen them starting to turn 18 (the same year the crime rate increases began). The sweet spot for criminal behavior seems to be the age range 18–24, both now and then (Blumstein, 2006). Fox (2006) points out that, in terms of those responsible for the most crime during this period, there was age, race, and gender effects. For example, he presents data demonstrating the following rank order of being most responsible for crime to least responsible: Black males, age 18–24, White males, age 18–24, Black males, age 14–17, and White males, age 14–17. This race effect was particularly pronounced in big cities, where the gap between White and Black crime was growing. This race based crime variation was pushed, too, by the large unemployment rate for African Americans. The already large proportioned unemployment rate for African Americans of two to one (compared to White Americans) in the 1960s continued to increase.

Such economic changes in the 1960s might also have played a part in the crime surge's etiology. Walker (2011), for example, points out that, while the economy may have had the verisimilitude of being healthy, there was, in fact, a "steady erosion in the availability of the industrial jobs that had been the traditional entry point into the labor market [of cities]" (p. 201). Although the relationship between crime and the economy is poorly understood, that such a positive correlation exists is indisputable. Blumstein and Wallman (2006), in summarizing the literature on the crime surge, posit a complex etiology consisting of increasing and new drug use, a rise in handgun ownership, demographic changes, and a push toward rehabilitation paradigms with little to no value. Once the surge started, it seemed to take on an endogenous quality—what Walker (2011) labeled as a contagion effect: As the surge caught momentum, criminal behavior became normalized, and subsequently amoralized. Thus, more people exhibited criminal behavior.

This crime surge, like the crime drop in the 1990s, was not a uniquely American phenomenon. But (and again, like the American crime drop), its magnitude was uniquely American (Walker, 2011; Zimring, 2008). The implications of the American crime surge were also, in a sense, quite unique, owing to the American system of federalism and dual party politics. For one, the crime surge pushed crime to the American public's attention, and politicians were all too eager to grab on to it as a political selling point. The year this became a part of the presidential platform was the 1964 election between Lyndon Johnson and Barry Goldwater (Walker, 2011). Crime has remained a selling point in politics ever since. The crime surge also played a part in leading to the President's Crime Commission and its influential publication *Crime in a Free Society*. This, as we have already seen, led to an increased federal influence over local policing by way of training, standards, and monies.

Finally, Zimring (2008) points out that the crime surge also led to Charles Silberman's hugely influential book on criminal justice, *Criminal Violence, Criminal Justice*, first published in 1978. Silberman's classic was the culmination of a six year project funded by the Ford Foundation through the Police Foundation, and it explored all aspects of American crime and its institutional response to deviance. It paid heavy attention to the issue of race and justice throughout the book, providing a sweeping historical and contemporary perspective. The title of his chapter introducing the section on the book about the now commonly called criminal justice *system* set the tenor for the entire section: "'The Insufficiency of Human Institutions': An Introduction to the Criminal Justice System." In his chapter on the police (also aptly titled "The Wisdom of Solomon, the Patience of Job: What the Police Do—and Don't Do"), he noted that the rising crime rate created a general discouragement about the ability of the police to affect any significant change. He concluded, rather starkly, with the recommendation that the United States needed to "abandon the quixotic faith that there is a police solution to the problem of criminal violence" (p. 341). Silberman's use of the term *quixotic* is interesting, as it denotes an ideal that is not just unrealistic and impractical, but one that strains all credulity and exceeds all ideals, implying that the police should never have gone down the road of professionalized crime fighting in the first place. As we have seen throughout the pages of this book, Silberman was merely giving voice to the era's *zeitgeist* about the police. Although his suggestion was somewhat hyperbolic, the perception that it expressed was not. This sort of sentiment only further harmed the relationship between the police and society and increased the us versus them attitude of line officers. It also pulled public support for local police behavior, largely justifying federal intervention.

Race riots and rising crime rates were not the only thing that contributed to the loss of public support and the increased federal interest in local policing: local *and* federal attention into the corrupt behavior of police officers and police agencies also aided this pattern. As I mentioned above, the rising crime rate was in many places excused by the presence of police corruption. As Weber first pointed out in the early 20th century, and as Tom Tyler (2006) would later articulate about the police specifically, people are only apt to obey the law insofar as they perceive its administration as just. It is therefore to a discussion of this unjust police behavior that I now turn.

POLICE CORRUPTION

Police corruption—no matter how uncommon or petty—is a serious concern for one straightforward reason: police are the only persons in the United States with the state sanctioned power to use lethal force against civilians, including United States citizens. Whenever that power is abused in any capacity, it threatens the Unites States' democratic principles as articulated under what is commonly referred to as due process. Although what constitutes corruption is difficult to nail down (and scholars don't necessarily agree on what constitutes corruption, a topic I take up below) this police power undergirds the actions of all officers (Bittner, 1970). The principled behavior of the police plays into the law abiding activities of citizens. To the extent that the police themselves do not "play by the rules," some people may feel that the rules do not apply to themselves, either. Corruption can result in the perpetuation of crime (as well as the creation of crime) and the deterioration of actual law enforcement.

These are only some of the effects of police misbehavior. For our purposes, we are especially interested in the effects of police behavior in terms of race and class, as these two issues were at the heart of the crime surge and the race riots. Generally, research in the 1970s revealed that both African Americans and those who lived in poorer neighborhoods held less positive opinions about the police. Jacob (1971), for example, found that Black civilians were more likely than their white counterparts to believe that police were *more* corrupt. He also found that Black civilians were likely to believe that police were more unfair, more harsh, less friendly, and crueler than white civilians. Bordua and Tifft (1971) found similar results and that Blacks were more angry and unhappy when they encountered the police than Whites. All of this was compounded in areas characterized as disadvantaged or of lower socioeconomic status.

What Does Police Corruption Look Like?

It is this divide, coupled with the majority-White make-up of police departments in the 1960s and 1970s, that was responsible, in part, for the race riots. As the corrupt practice of police agencies came to light in the 1960s and 1970s (and beyond), it became clear that it was detrimentally focused on Black and other minority citizens, and the neighborhoods they most commonly resided in. This behavior ran the gamut of what "corruption" actually looks like, a topic with considerable disagreement among policing scholars. When we talk about police corruption, we're essentially talking about police deviance—behavior that departs from the norm or standard. In this sense, corruption is actually a subset of what is referred to as police misconduct. It is fair to use the term "corruption" as it is the word most likely employed and thought of in the minds of lay persons.

What is and is not deviance in policing is truly a moving target. Kappeler and colleagues (1998), for example, point out at least four ways to measure and define police corruption: statistically, in the sense of the mean behavior; an absolutist moral perspective; a situational approach that relies strongly on community and agency norms and context; and what they call the normative approach. At least two things are clear from these definitions: first, that there is considerable overlap between the categories; and second, that the absolutist perspective notwithstanding, most ideas about what corruption is are rather fluid, implying that some behavior that may be immoral is not necessary corrupt. Kappeler and his colleagues (1998) and Sherman (1974) suggest that there is something more to corruption itself—namely, that it is predicated on the self-serving interests of the police officer. This is largely seen in the sort of things that were being treated as corruption in research contemporary to these definitions: taking bribes and extortion (although Sherman also includes sex on duty, sleeping on duty, drinking on duty, and perjury, foreshadowing what would essentially be a broadening of the definition of corruption that would come from the fallout of the Knapp Commission—see below).

"Causes" of Police Corruption

Whatever corruption "objectively" is, in practice it is often understood in the same terms that the United States Supreme Court once famously defined pornography: civilians know it when they see it. That's a very unfair ontology, but a very real one. It is appropriate to also point out that the etiology of corruption is largely as mysterious as its definition. Nevertheless, researchers have come to agree on some broad covariate categories. Almost all researchers, since the 1960s, agree that the erstwhile "rotten apples" explanation was bunk. This theory, popular among police defenders during the initial run of the public's exposure to police corruption in the early 20th century, placed the blame of corrupt police behavior squarely on the shoulders of the officer. Barker (1977) called this approach a myth, and Sherman (1974) used equally strong language when he wrote that the cause of police corruption is best understood as a "painful process of choices, and not because they [the police] are pathological 'rotten apples'" (p. 191). By "painful process of choices," Sherman was alluding to a slippery slope explanation. For example, an officer may start out with only partially enforcing the law, and then begin "picking up loot" at the scene of a burglary. For Sherman, then, police corruption was not *just* a slippery slope, but a slippery slope in the context of very specific social forces.

Most scholars who study police corruption have spent the bulk of their time trying to disentangle and understand these social forces involved in the process of police corruption. Barker (1977), for example, suggested that corruption was the result of opportunity, socialization, and peer group support for corrupt behavior. Chambliss (1971), too, noted the importance of the policing peer group, suggesting that the us versus them culture of policing, with its accompanying code of silence, only served to reinforce corrupt behavior among officers. To this internal mix, Chambliss (1971) also added external elements that might be associated with corruption. These external elements include the relationship between the police, local businesses, and city politics. He even went so far as to compare this triad of corruption to organized crime.

As I have said elsewhere (Cooper, 2014), the etiology of police behavior is understatedly complex. This statement applies to corrupt police behavior to an even greater degree than routine police work. To wit, in her chapter on the "Causes and Correlates of Police Corruption" from her exhaustive book *Fallen Blue Knights*, Sanja Ivkovic (2005) lists and details over two dozen internal and external factors, including: individual factors, like an officer's propensity toward corruption; the paramilitary bureaucratic setup of police agencies; a lack of real-time supervision for line officers; and weak (even impotent) external mechanisms of external control. She writes at the beginning of this chapter that there is a "remarkably heterogeneous set of causes and correlates of police corruption and the complex relations among them" (p. 64). Indeed. Sherman (1974) too provides a complex path diagram of police behavior or corruption that begins with the interrelationship between *community structure, legal opportunities,* and *organizational characteristics.* These in turn influence the extent of police corruption both directly and indirectly through various *control mechanisms*, which are themselves endogenously related to the antecedent covariates (see p. 38). Like Ivkovic, Sherman, writing over thirty years prior, managed to "sum" up the state of police corruption research with an extensive litany of causes.

Although early intervention/warning systems are becoming common today, and draw on this corpus of research to prevent corrupt behavior, brutality, and abuse (Walker, 2005), these systems still rely on an associations approach to prediction, that is, one based on risk factors. We still do not fully understand why certain officers and groups of officers break public trust by engaging in corrupt behavior. The questions that scholars—and the public—sought regarding corruption in the 1960s largely remain constant today.

Corruption during the 1960s and 1970s

All of this talk begs the question, what was going on that got researchers so interested in the misbehavior of police in the first place? Initial research into police corruption was incredibly journalistic and sensational, often based on an "informant" (Barker, 1977). It was not until the 70s that we started to see empirical work coming out of the universities that systematically explored corruption. While the definition of what constituted *corrupt* behavior was still evolving, researchers tended to focus on two specific forms of immoral and unlawful police behavior: the taking of bribes and involving themselves with vice crime. Sherman (1974), for one, found that accepting bribes was often the entry point to greater corrupt behavior. As noted above, the interdependent relationship between city politics, the police, and private businesses, as articulated by Chambliss (1971), was based largely in vice crimes.

In Rubinstein's (1973) participant study of the Philadelphia police, he too noted that much of the immoral behavior that the police undertook was focused on vice. His experience and observations reflect the etiological discussion above:

> The obligation to enforce the vice laws presents the police with insoluble dilemmas. Regardless of what system a department uses...or the degree of freedom a commissioner has from political interference, the department administration must constantly struggle to control the inclinations of some to exploit their opportunities for graft...[But many] of the illegal things that policemen do are not designed to generate payoffs for them but to meet obligations established by the department. If the patrolman were freed from having to make vice arrests, only the corrupt and the money hungry, would continue to do the illegal things so many policemen do. There are no legal ways to enforce the drug laws on the streets, so any pressure on the police to make more drug arrests is an open encouragement to them to lie and violate their pledge to uphold the Constitution. (p. 376ff)

Rubinstein essentially found that police work *cum* police work not only encourages but *requires* immoral behavior. Whether that behavior is corrupt is only part of the issue: "The patrolman is obliged to violate the law, degrade people, lie, and even shame himself in his own eyes in order to make arrests he knows are meaningful and he suspects produce money for others" (p. 400). There is nothing illegal about all of those acts—but each can be understood as being immoral. This has implications both for the police and for their relationship with the public. It can, for example, corrode the trust the public may have had for the police. This can lead to further criminal behavior on the part of civilians, who no longer view them as the enforcers of the law—and therefore the law itself—as legitimate (Tyler, 2006).

In terms of the police, this can lead to more seriously corrupt behavior, and to a dangerous level of cynicism (Neiderhoffer, 1969; Rubinstein, 1973). Skolnick (1982), for example, found that police were more willing to deceive civilians during an investigation, and progressively less willing to do so during interrogation and the courtroom processes. He also found that whether an officer was willing to lie under testimony, that is, was willing to perjure himself, largely depended on whether that officer was willing to lie during investigations. Even those officers who may not lie under oath may tacitly accept other officers' deceptions as being necessary and almost all officers will remain silent about this sort of behavior. Skolnick (1982) too points out that this creates a paradox for the police wherein to enforce the law—a codified, moral standard—they must lie. Or, said otherwise, to get at the truth they must avoid the truth.

The resulting cognitive dissonance that this paradox must create for the police, along with the consequential rationalizing away of this ambivalence and the damaged relationship between the police and civilians that corruption can cause, were brought to light during the 1970s with the famous Knapp Commission's report, which can also be viewed as the final nail in the coffin of the professional policing model.

The Knapp Commission

The Knapp Commission's unoriginal complete title sums up just what it was all about: "The Commission to Investigate Allegations of Police Corruption and the City's Anti-Corruption Procedures". The mayor of New York (John Lindsay) formed the Commission in 1970 after newspaper reports began surfacing about widespread corruption in the NYPD, especially in the Special Investigations Unit. These claims were the result of two whistleblowers, Frank Serpico and David Durk. The commission, lead by its namesake Judge Whitman Knapp, included three years of investigations and public hearings. One of the most important things that came out of the whistle-blowing was the appointment of Patrick Murphy as police commissioner. Murphy was given the mandate to "clean things up". Murphy would become one of the most important leaders of police reform, whose influence is yet felt today through the Police Executive Research Forum, as well as through numerous collaborations with scholars and other police reformers.

The Commission's final report was released to the public in 1973, and it covered every topic imaginable. Their conclusions were damning and universal in the sense that they uncovered corruption throughout the NYPD, at every level, and using every medium, from gambling to vice. The report enumerated almost twenty examples of specific corrupt behavior. Some behavior was relatively benign, such as storing drug paraphernalia used during regular police operations in personal lockers. Other behavior was more serious—indeed, more terrifying, such as kidnapping potential witnesses to prevent trial testimony. Much of the corruption had to do with extorting drug deals and gambling rings, often by plain clothes units. There was tacit acceptance of this behavior among almost all officers, whether they felt "ok" with this sort of behavior or not. Although corruption complaints would surface from time to time, internally (from within the ranks of the NYPD) they were summarily swept under the rug and protected from public purview by the blue code of silence. As a result of Knapp's public hearings and investigations, even before the commission completed its report, numerous NYPD personnel and officers were indicted on charges dealing with corruption.

Another way that the Knapp Commission's report has made a lasting impact on policing in general was in its description of some officers as "grass eaters" and others as "meat eaters." According to the report, grass eaters are those who accept certain perquisites that are not necessarily condoned by the department—such as bribes, free lunches, etc. Meat eaters, on the other hand, seek such opportunities out, using extortion, blackmail, burglary, etc. Importantly, even though (as the report argued) most officers who engage in corrupt behavior would be placed in the grass eaters category, such officers *must* remain silent about the behavior of the more nefarious meat eaters. To expose the meat eaters risks exposing themselves and breaks the code of silence, which may result in being ostracized altogether.

The Knapp Commission's report, and all of its open hearings, revealed to an American public that corruption was *not* the fruit of a few bad apples; rather, it was systemic—in some cases prolifically so—and selfish. There was little noble about it. The image of the professional American policeman was—forever—shattered, not only in the minds of minority communities, but now even the minds of White Americans. This image was itself advanced by the police, as Skolnick and Fyfe (1993, p. xi) show in the opening quote to their book on police and the excessive use of force:

> The television program *Dragnet* was one of the great instruments to give the people of the United States a picture of the policeman as he really is. It was most authentic. We participated in the editing of the scripts and in their filming. If we had any objections on technical grounds our objections were met. This program showed the true portrait of the policeman as a hard-working, selfless man, willing to go out and brave all sorts of hazards and work long hours to protect the community.

This was William Parker, chief of the LA Police, speaking in 1962. The title to Skolnick and Fyfe's prologue speaks volumes: "Whatever Happened to *Dragnet*?" In short: it was shattered by the Knapp Commission and subsequent blue ribbon commissions. The gap between *Dragnet* and *The Wire* also speaks volumes about where America is now in terms of their image of the police and corruption. The Knapp Commission was, to borrow a Biblical turn of phrase, both the culmination and the beginning of woes for the police out of the morass of the 1950s, 1960s and 1970s.

CONCLUSIONS

The rising crime rate and the public's awareness of this rising crime rate could not come at a worse time for the police, in that it occurred in tandem with explosive, systematic police corruption across the nation. So not only were the police viewed as ineffective, they were understood to be nothing short of a moral liability. This shifted the focus onto the police by the public, politicians, and academics. As Sherman (1974) pointed out, it was the recognition of police corruption that, more than anything, kick-started scholarly interest in the police. This research would itself turn its attention to other policing subjects, eventually tearing down the illusion that the professional model was effective at fighting crime. In fact, it was simply harmful.

Predictably, all this attention to police corruption led to a number of reform recommendations—among which the Knapp Commission's report led the pack. But as is always the case for any public institution, reform is often more a matter of window dressing than the hard work of organizational change. Herman Goldstein, famous for his policing innovations and particularly for the development of problem oriented policing, wrote a book in 1977 titled *Policing a Free Society*. This was obviously a play on the President's Commission's 1960s publication *Challenge of Crime in a Free Society*. Goldstein eloquently outlined the difficulties of maintaining an inherently un-democratic police force in a society that espouses democratic ideals. In commenting on the response *du jour* to police malfeasance, Goldstein noted that citizen groups and complaint systems were viewed by police as emanating from criminals, thus undermining their very purpose. Indeed, Goldstein argued, the very *nature* of police work and organization precluded any meaningful input from the public. Policing was adversarial by nature, because routinized task behaviors create insensitivity among officers, the blue code of silence, a fear verging on the paranoia of tort liability, and a work environment characterized by duplicity and hypocrisy; all combined to create not just the fields from which the United States reaped the race riots of the 1960s, but also created an atmosphere where any public input about the police was viewed with suspicion and hostility by the police.

It was clear to Goldstein then, and it is clear to most police commentators today—lay and sworn alike—that before the police could be expected to do anything about crime, they would have to be seen as legitimate in the eyes of the public they served. Before that could happen, corruption would need to be weeded out. The old defense of a "few bad apples" would have to go. Rather, as Goldstein urged in 1977, police wrong-doing of all sorts needed to be reframed as an agency problem. *Policing* needed to be reframed. Through a number of trials and errors, and some successes, policing would, over the next forty years, begin to transform itself. This transformation, while not problem-free by any stretch of the imagination, was nevertheless something that could interact at a meaningful level, with the environment, and could have a meaningful and positive impact on the crime rate. This is the topic of the next chapter: how policing today is largely the result of institutional corrections geared toward preventing the mistakes and consequences of the 1950s, 1960s, and 1970s.

Chapter Nine

What Professional Policing *Then* Means for 21st Century Policing *Now*

Four overlapping themes should be apparent from the last seven chapters. First, as demonstrated by the rising crime rate and the increasing amount of social science research, the promises of the professional movement to turn police into expert crime fighters and thereby make America a safer place had not come to fruition. On the contrary, all signs pointed toward police causing more harm than good. Second, lawsuits, whistleblowing, research, journalism, and political interference each contributed to the outing of American police corruption. This added to the sentiment that the police were not only ineffective, but inefficient (to say the least). Third, the police were not communicating—in any sense of the word—with the public. This was especially prominent for minority communities. The lack of communication was due, in part to the fourth theme, isolation. The us versus them attitude of the American police was written into the professional model. Its purpose was to preclude political corruption from infiltrating the police as it had in the late 1800s and early 1900s. It did this, but it also had the unfortunate consequence of exasperating *all* of the problems between the police and society during these three decades.

These four themes are clearly related to each other. They are offered here merely as an organizing heuristic, and should not be understood as definitive or mutually exclusive. Their impacts can only be understood holistically as an emergent property of policing and society. These themes led to more reforms that, slowly over the course of three decades, have changed policing in terms of its form and its function. I suggest three results that, again, while discussed individually must be fully understood as a whole. First, science would become intimately involved in reforming the nature of the police. Given the role of social science in tearing the image of the police down, it seems rather appropriate. This manifested not only in terms of social scientists studying the police (both as university and in-house researchers) but also in terms of new approaches to line-officer functions and policing technology. Second, new accountability methods were developed to reduce corruption and improve the involvement of the public in the *quotidien* business of the police. Third, and at the heart of the problems between the police and the public in the 50s, 60s, and 70s, was a new (some might argue, renewed) focus on the community.

This chapter ties all of these themes together, connecting policing *then* with policing *now*. To this end, I first briefly review the policing themes of the 50s, 60s, and 70s, and then follow up by discussing those policing themes that followed and that represent contemporary policing. But policing has not completed the change–and nor has society. Therefore, I also discuss several things about policing that remain problematic for the relationship between police and society. This is especially pertinent given, for example, the events in Ferguson, Missouri of 2014. Finally, I consider two examples of contemporary policing that demonstrate just how much policing has changed in form and function, as well as in terms of its relationship with the community *and* with other justice agencies. I conclude with a conversation about what to do about the "police mandate" given all that the last eight chapters have suggested.

POLICING *THEN*

As indicated in the introduction, four themes emerged in the decades of the 50s, 60s, and 70s that led the police *out* of the professional model: effectiveness, efficiency, communication, and social isolation. These four themes have been explored extensively throughout the pages of this book. The purpose of the current section is merely to review these themes in anticipation of the main focus of the chapter—namely, the consequences of these themes. The professional model's focus on form and function over results, coupled with its closed-model approach to the world outside of policing played an unduly influential part in the incredibly disruptive years of these three decades.

Perhaps the most damning "wake up call"—both to the police and to the American *body politic*—was the rising crime rate. If the police were expert crime fighters they should be able to do something about crime by using the very model that proclaimed them as professional crime fighters. This was clearly not the case, particularly in the 1970s. Even in the 1960s it was becoming clear that something was happening to the crime rate and that police had very little to do with it (at least, in any positive sense). In the 1970's, when the crime rate's increase can only be described as "sudden," police—who were already in the crosshairs of an angry nation because of the civil rights movement—came under severe empirical scrutiny. Not only was the occasional sociologist interested in the police, but an entire academic discipline, criminal justice, was devoted to critically examining their outputs. The research that resulted from these scholars only reinforced what the rising crime rate seemed to be implying: what the police did, did nothing to "fight" crime. On the contrary, police actions often served to exacerbate crime.

This growing body of research also unveiled another element of policing that immediately and, some might argue, irredeemably, tarnished the image of the police: systematic corruption at almost all levels of an agency, and throughout the United States. The publicity that this corruption received severely damaged the notion that police were corrupt in isolation. Instead, it became apparent that the police's problem with corruption was deeper and much more organizational than previously acknowledged. More generally, this is part of a larger picture of police *misbehavior*, which can be conceptualized as inefficiency, at best, or gross constitutional negligence, at worse. Indeed, it was this latter category that the courts in the 50s and 60s had in mind when they laid down a number of procedural laws all geared toward limiting police officer discretion and constitutional misapprobation. Under the Warren Court's due process revolution, the police began to feel pressure from both sides of the spectrum—public and policymakers—to change their behavior. As we shall soon see, courtroom "interference" would reach its peak in the 80s and 90s with a handful of consent decrees that would be slapped on a number of large, nationally known police departments.

At the heart of so many of these problems was the lack of communication between the police and civilians, especially minority citizens. This communication deficiency was due in large part to the historically poor relationship between minorities and the police. A large amount of baggage can accrue between the police and minorities when the former were created to keep the latter in check, both in the North and the South. But this problem was only part of the picture of poor communication between police and minorities. The professional model itself, as already indicated, provided the organizational means to prevent real communication. It was not just communication between the police and citizens that lacked, it was also communication between the police and other criminal justice agencies. This aspect of communication came to a head when the new systems approach to the administration of justice became popular. The police were now "flanked" on all sides: civilians, the courts, scholars, the press, politicians, and other criminal justice actors.

All of this led to a very intense sense of isolation that was only reinforced by the inherent conservatism of the police. Isolation, lack of communication, and a functional inability to adapt coupled with an ideological propensity that precluded change lit the fuse that would ignite the bomb known as the "Long

Hot Summers" of the 1960s. City after city and year after year, people experienced violent race riots, resulting in death, injury, and millions of dollars in property damage. At their nadir, and in the face of their conservatism and bureaucratic protections, the police would *have* to change. The process would be incredibly slow and have a number of fits and starts. Eventually, however, the police *did* change—in both form and function.

POLICING *NOW*

As chapter two points out, and any passing knowledge of the history of policing will reveal, police *have* changed prior to the 1960s. Of course, some of those changes (e.g., professionalization) were not necessarily for the better. The professional movement may have stemmed *political* corruption, but it allowed for *departmental* corruption and ultimately facilitated the fall of bureaucratic policing. In fact, many of the problems experienced in the 50s, 60s, and 70s were *not* new to police. Policing had been "reformed" in response to many of these problems before, particularly corruption and the relationship between police and citizens. Why, then, did things not really *change* until the 80s and later? Why were these three decades the "tipping point"? And why did change take *so long*?

In his highly important book, *The New World of Police Accountability*, Walker (2005) summarizes how the traditional approaches (including the blue ribbon commissions covered in the pages of this book) simply didn't work. First, the technology grew too fast for the police bureaucracy to keep up. Thus there were never any established principles of managing motorized patrol. There was no way to really hold line officers accountable for breaching the law or the constitution in general, and what guidelines there were, were either weak or weakly enforced. While private companies began looking at how to manage civil litigation liability (often through firing problem employees), the police stubbornly held on to and protected "their own". Walker (2005) also notes that although criminally prosecuting police officers was tried on occasion, it was rarely effective (although *case law* through the United States Supreme Court did seem to have an impact). Walker also points out that despite their sweeping condemnation and in-depth research, blue ribbon commissions were, at the end of the day, politically impotent. The result was that any reforms made in the immediate aftermath of the 60s was largely window dressing that failed to reach line officers. What changes were made were never institutionalized, in part because they utterly ignored the role of supervisors and ways to make citizen oversight effective.

To a certain degree, the lack of long-term change was due to the form of policing. The professional model is sometimes called the bureaucratic model for a reason: it is a bureaucracy. By design, bureaucracies are resistant to change, in part because they are *not* designed to handle input from the external environment very well. But we can't place all the blame on the bureaucratizing of the police. The professional model also encouraged (and Vollmer was particularly keen on this) the adoption of new technologies. While new technology allowed the police to be more accessible to the public, it also changed *how* they approached crime control. By waiting on calls from the public through telephone calls (and later through the new 911 system), the police moved from a Peelian preventive approach to one that can best be described as reactive. And with the introduction of motorized patrol, gone were the informal contacts and familiarity with neighborhood residents that was possible with foot patrol (Reiss, 1992). The new focus on technology use pulled police away from the public while it introduced the police into the most intimate moments of civilian's lives. It allowed the police to cover an enormous amount of territory, while simultaneously removing the need for the traditional station house. Now, all police could report, via automobile, to central station houses, further removing the police yet another step from civilians and neighborhoods. With the increase of police in numbers came specialized bureaus who were specialized over *crimes* not *places*, and thus utterly disconnected from the people whom they served (Reiss, 1992).

The impact of technology on the police is now largely taken for granted. Dash cams, TASER's and other electrical conductive devices, GPS, and license plate reading technologies are now par for the course. But scholars as early as the 60s and 70s could see that, more than anything, technology was going to be the true harbinger of change. Some researchers, such as Peter Manning, largely built their career on exploring what, exactly, technology meant for the relation of the police and society. Although technology initially harmed this relationship, it would be the gateway to more "civilian friendly" practices, including community oriented and problem oriented policing; however, technology would also continue to harm the relationship between police and society by allowing for intense and real-time data gathering and analysis that would reduce civilian and crime to simple data, as with COMPSTAT and zero-tolerance policing. As will be discussed further below, technology has been somewhat of a two-edged sword for the police throughout their history together.

Data itself has had a rough relationship with the police ever since the FBI took over the International Association of Chiefs of Police's *Uniform Crime Report*. Operationalizing police activity in any way that meaningfully captures what they are both doing and trying to do has never really been successful. On the contrary, it has tended to force police to look upon citizens and places as numbers and quotas, further dehumanizing their work. As Samuel Walker (2007) has pointed out, police wear multiple hats, and often the roles that these hats assume are contradictory. This can lead to very unfair expectations of the police in general, and when these expectations are enforced numerically, it is a design for failure. Again, Skolnick and Fyfe (1993), quoting an officer, called this pattern for what it was: the fucking numbers game.

The fact of the matter is that such "traditional" measures rarely capture exactly what the police are trying to do—which itself may differ from situation to situation. Traditional measures focus on arrests rates, calls for service, and response time. But most of the time, police are doing things *other* than law enforcement, such as order maintenance (Wilson, 1968). This means that things like community sentiment toward the police, neighborhood fear of crime, and peer evaluations become just as important—if not more—than crime counts. Even these measures fail to fully appreciate the complex relationship between the police and society, and often come to loggerheads with the role of police as crime fighters. Resolving the new realization of how complex the police role is (perhaps "renewed" is a better term, given the research of Rubinstein and others in the 60s and 70s) with the need to evaluate their performance in a criminal justice system governed by the term "evidenced-based" has been a major catalyst for change in the last three decades.

Changes

Evidenced-Based Work

Evidenced-based practices, like the professionalism movement of the early 20th century, is not relegated to the justice field. Indeed, it appears to have started in medicine (Buysse & Wesley, 2006). The term "evidenced-based" has become so popular in governance that, like the "total quality management" of the 1980s and 1990s, I worry that it risks becoming trivialized. What "evidenced-based" means varies from agency to agency, yet there are some commonalities among most definitions. Returning to its medical roots, I prefer the definition offered by Arizona State University's Center for the Advancement of Evidenced-Based Practice, which is housed in the College of Nursing & Health Innovation:

> Evidence-based practice facilitates the integration of internal evidence (i.e., quality and outcome data), external evidence (i.e., research) and practice across multiple settings to improve patient, provider, community, and system outcomes.

If we replace *patient* with *suspect/defendant/convict/victim*, etc., then this definition neatly sums up what evidenced-based is all about. Then-director of the National Institute of Justice (NIJ) John Laub (2012) invoked the ethos of evidenced-based practices when he talked about the need to create a "culture of science" at the NIJ:

What we need to do is create a culture of science and research within the institute. And what I'd like to see happen is that we as an institute embrace science...for me what that means is embracing empirical data, embracing transparency, and also embracing a critical perspective...The idea of a science is to challenge: challenge conventional wisdom, challenge what people think is right, and to be able to develop a critical skeptical attitude...For people who are actually creating the science, that is going to be also for them, I think, also a part of an intellectual pursuit to create the best science possible, that's rigorous, and, as I've said repeatedly, that's of importance to the field at large..It's both a process, as well as a substance, in terms of what it means to be...an agency that embraces science and what it means to develop a culture of science within the agency.

Evidenced-based practices can therefore be understood not as a basic science (although that, too, has its place) but as an applied social science. It is more than even this: it is an applied science that is embedded not only in the daily practice of the police (to return to the issue at hand), but that is embedded in their mission and mandate. Perhaps the turning point for the usefulness of this idea came not after the damning research of the 1970s, but after Lawrence Sherman published his 1992 study on directed patrol, which demonstrated how science can help police successfully reduce crime. In short, Sherman found that while traditional (read: random) patrol had no impact on crime, directing police patrol to specific places at specific times for specific types of crime—all of which were defined by carefully and relatively rigorous scientific research—*could* reduce those crimes in those places.

What's more, this answered a perennial question for scholars and practitioners alike: could science be timely enough to matter for the police (Skogan, 2010)? The answer was and remains *yes*, insofar as research is embedded in the police department and researchers, police officers, and administrators understand the limits and time constraints that both parties regularly face. Science is traditionally time consuming, and practitioners have usually looked upon it as prolix, at best, and irrelevant, at worst. This changed dramatically and swiftly with the advent of powerful and affordable computer systems. As soon as computers were moved from warehouses to offices (and later to patrol cars), research became timely. The issue of timeliness would only improve as statistical software became more user friendly and statistics became better known among police administrators. Although there are still important hurdles to overcome in terms of police-researcher relationships, the reality is that we have moved beyond talking about it to expectedly doing it.

Walker (2011) agrees with this claim, and points out that criminal justice is actually a late comer to the evidenced-based world (which, given all that I have discussed in this book, should come as no surprise). It is, he argues, the "new standard" of crime policy (p. 9). He points to at least two events in support of this contention. First, in 2003, the Department of Justice (DOJ) created the Coalition for Evidenced-Based Policy to promote the adoption and improvement of evidenced-based justice, including policing. In doing so, the DOJ borrowed heavily from the United Kingdom Home Office's own approach to situational crime prevention (in an eerie throwback to the USA's copy-catting of the Kingdom of Britain's model of urban policing in the 1820s). And second, was the founding of the Campbell Collaboration in 2000 (named after famous sociological methodologist Donald Campbell), whose mission is to provide meta-analyses of rigorous experimental and quasi-experimental studies of specific crime policies—many of which having to do with policing.

The Campbell Collaboration lays out the standards for evidenced-based crime policies. As outlined by Walker (2011), policies and practices must:

• have empirical evidence of effectiveness
• such evidence must be based on experiments or quasi-experiments
• there must be numerous studies, demonstrating replicable results

For anyone familiar with criminal justice research, these are *all* high benchmarks, given criminologists' and criminal justicians' love of measures of association and one-shot case studies. But this serves only to highlight just how seriously the justice system as a whole—and especially the police—are taking evidenced-based work. Unlike the 1950s, research is no longer seen as the enemy, but a valuable, and, in many cases, an absolutely necessary ally.

Problem-Oriented Policing

One of the most innovative ways that research has found its way into policing is through *problem-oriented policing* (POP). This tactic is unique because it involves line officers directly by redefining both their role and what they do. Initially outlined by the enormously influential policing scholar Herman Goldstein in a 1979 article, POP came into its own after his 1990 book was published under the appropriately titled *Problem-Oriented Policing*. From the start, Goldstein set out to improve policing by redefining how they approached crime. Rather than *reacting* to crime, he argued that police needed to take steps to solve persistent community problems. To do so, the police needed to do more than arrest criminals. Arresting criminals was merely treating the symptoms, so to speak. Instead, the police needed to focus on the underlying conditions. Line officers were those closest to the problems and were therefore in the best position to understand and work toward solving these problems.

To uncover the underlying conditions, Goldstein suggested that police focus less on going from call to call and focus more on *what locations specific* crimes were occurring, in order to uncover geographic patterns of crime. To assist in this focus, he offered up what is called the SARA model: scan, analyze, respond, and assess. This means that the police can *scan* for specific problems, and *analyze* them to better understand their causes. Once the causes are understood, the police *respond* with a solution tailored to that situation, and then *assess* how well their response worked. If it did not work, then they returned to the *analyze* stage. The SARA model is clearly the wolf of the scientific method in sheep's clothing, distilled in such a way that it was applicable to the police.

POP is usually presented alongside the so-called crime triangle. The crime triangle suggests that a crime event takes place whenever a motivated offender comes into contact with a suitable target in the absence of a capable guardian. It further suggests that if the police can *remove* one of those elements then they can prevent the crime. Notice that the crime triangle is not focused on the *criminal* (that is, on the motivated offender), but on the *crime event*. By shifting the focus from the offender to the event, POP pushes the police away from reactive methods to more preventive methods. Importantly, the crime triangle, and by extension POP, is premised on Felson's (cf. Cohen & Felson, 1979) Routine Activities Theory. The implications of this are almost more important than their actual application: a sociological *theory* can inform policing *practices* in a way that directly applies to the line officer.

Relatively speaking, POP seems to have been widely (and readily) adopted by the police in the United States. Although we have no good data on exactly how many departments have adopted POP, we do have some anecdotal evidence that indicates its popularity. Specifically, from 1993-2007, the Police Executive Research Forum has awarded the "Herman Goldstein Award for Excellence in Problem-Oriented Policing." It is currently awarded by the Center for Problem-Oriented Policing. This is a highly competitive and prestigious award, with about 60 entries per year across the nation. Since 1993, there have been over 600 entries. One of the reasons POP has "worked" so well in the last few decades is because of computer mapping software and statistics. I now turn to the technological innovations that can also be traced, at least in part, to the events of the 50s, 60s, and 70s.

Technology

These three decades demonstrate two things to us about technology. First, that it can have unintended and negative results rather than the positive and intended outcomes with which they were first adopted. Second, that technology can have an incredible impact not just on the function of the police, but on their form (Reiss, 1992). The key changes that came out of these negative impacts were focused on minimizing the bad and increasing the good. This may sound simplistic, but it is nevertheless accurate: police turned to technology with an eye toward utility *without* sacrificing public relationships. (As we shall see, though, this does not always work out.) The role of technology, for the police, has always been just as symbolic as it was practical. Manning (1992), for example, notes

> Technology is not only a physical and material matter, it takes on intersubjective meaning, consequence, purpose, use, impact, direction, or social significance in social and organizational contexts in which collective lines of action are articulated. (p. 353)

That's a bit of a mouthful, but what Manning is suggesting is that technology changes how information is processed and how decisions are made, which directly impacts the relationship between civilians and the police. Thus, just as patrol cars and fingerprinting procured the myth of police-as-expert-crime-fighters in the 1920s, so too does computers and crime mapping (*inter alia*) maintain this myth among the police and the body politic. The biggest difference between *then* and *now* is not the symbolism, then, but the utility of technology.

In the same chapter, Manning (1992) suggests three domains where technology has changed considerably for the police: information, intelligence, and operations. That is, technology has changed—has improved—for the police in terms of the ability to get information of all sorts, the ability to consume and interpret that information, and the ability to transform that information into meaningful policies and practices. Thus, it is not surprising that he argues that the most important technology innovations for the police include computers and software. Walker and Katz (2011) agree, pointing out numerous examples of how computers and software have been made to work for the police in ingenious ways, including: computer aided dispatch, mobile computing in patrol cars, license plate readers, and face recognition. Additionally, technology has improved less-than-lethal weapons, such as those produced by TASER, International. TASER has itself led the technocratic police movement by placing cameras on their TASERS and uploading video and other data to a proprietary cloud. Video has become increasingly typical of police officers, who now have cameras mounted on the dashboard of their vehicles, on their shoulders, and their sunglasses.

All this brings us back to Manning's (1992) contention that technology has changed how police respond to and interact with civilians—both as individual officers and as an organization. Reiss (1992), in the same volume, agreed, noting that technology has allowed the police to meaningfully move from being reactive to being preventive. This has been accomplished in large part by the advancements in spatial computing; to wit, the advent and improvement of *crime mapping*, a rather nebulous term for a number of mapping techniques for tracking, discerning, and preventing crime and mobilizing police resources. *Crime analysis* has become more than thinking smartly about crime or undercover work that develops networks of narcs. It has evolved into sophisticated, statistical, tactical, and strategic thinking (Walker & Katz, 2011). Perhaps nowhere has this become more *real* than with the popular COMPSTAT program—although it, too, has come with a price paid by the minority community.

COMPSTAT is the brainchild of the New York Police Department, specifically of William Bratton, who began as the head of the transit authority and ended as the police commissioner of the entire NYPD. COMPSTAT (short for *computer statistics*) combines timely crime mapping with the aggressive enforcement of low level offenses, typically called zero-tolerance policing. The idea behind zero-tolerance policing is that by focusing on low level crimes, which are usually very public, police can net more serious criminals. Where COMPSTAT comes in is showing supervisors where which crimes are occurring. Although there are several variations on the New York model, the typical pattern is for supervisors to go over the statistics, together, with command, where they go over current strategies and consider new strategies. Some COMPSTAT meetings behave like brainstorming, problem-solving sessions. Others, however, are more similar to shaming rituals for those supervisors whose areas are not living up to expectations. Regardless, there is some, albeit limited, empirical evidence that COMPSTAT actually does reduce crime (whether it is or is not coupled with zero-tolerance policing). For example, when coupled with hot spots policing it seems to reduce specific crimes in specific areas. Rosenfeld, Fornango, and Baumer (2005), however, found almost no support for the impact of COMPSTAT and zero-tolerance policing. What *has* been uncovered, however, is an astronomical increase in complaints against the police in New York *because* of these two innovations and several civil rights lawsuits against the NYPD for discrimination against blacks and Latinos. In other words, technology remains a dangerous "weapon" and continues, in some circumstances, to deteriorate the relationship between minorities and the police.

Accountability Mechanisms

Technology has also been front and center in terms of innovations in holding police accountable. Given that police behavior vis-a-vis crime can be understood as reactive during the three decades under consideration in this book, it should be no surprise that accountability processes were also reactive. That is, police behavior could only be held in check *if* they did something. There was no way to "preemptively" deal with a "problem police officer." It was not just the reactive nature of police accountability that rendered it so ineffective in the 50s, 60s, and 70s. The "traditional" practices simply did not work, if they were implemented, at all. As Walker (2005) writes, the police needed "new strategies and tools for dealing with the ancient problem of police misconduct" (p. 3). Such strategies would necessitate changes at the level of organization and, again, to no one's surprise, changes in the relationships between police and the community.

This changed with the advent of technology in policing. The ability to collect real time data about police behavior allowed supervisors to uncover behavior patterns that regularly led to more serious misconduct. This has provided supervisors with the opportunity to correct such behavior before it spiraled out of control. Using new and real-time computer database technology, agencies shifted to a system of "early interventions," whereby certain red flag indicators would catch a supervisor's attention, who could then meet with the officer in question and work out a plan of remediation and improvement. Such early intervention systems have shown extreme promise to curbing police misconduct (Walker, 2005; Walker, Alpert, & Kenney, 2001). Police agencies have also improved how civilians are included in the accountability process. While internal affairs divisions and inter-departmental oversight remain common, citizen oversight committees and ombudsmen are also common in today's police agencies (White, 2007). Although the degree to which such citizen oversight has an actual say in cases of police misconduct varies—as does their ability to elicit change—it is simply no longer the case that citizens are *not* part of the process. In other words, the police have learned the importance of listening to civilian voices, even in the most sensitive and "bluest" of cases.

Police accountability remains a struggle for law enforcement in America. As Walker (2005) put it, "it is a basic principle of a democratic society that the police should be answerable to the public" (p. 8). But *how* remains a perennial problem. Walker goes on to point out that police don't *want* to be scrutinized, and that the public can't really understand the highly situational occurrences of police misconduct—real or perceived. This is all complicated by the historically poor relationship between the police and the minority community. Even if a police officer is doing the right thing by the books, if he is doing it in a community rife with racialized tension, it may only serve to fan the flames of civil unrest. It is for this reason that the simplistic "PR" campaigns of the 1970s and 1980s failed so miserably to do anything for the rapport between police and minority communities: they were too simplistic. But this relationship *has* seen marked improvement over the last four decades. Granted, such improvement has been largely place-based, but even this is an improvement given the very localized nature of American policing. It is to this final topic of changes in policing that I *now* turn.

Community

More than any other topic—and for reasons that should now be painfully obvious to the reader—*community* has been the *leitmotif* for law enforcement for the last forty (or more) years. Consider the chapter titles of Glensor, Correia, and Peak's 2000 book on community and policing, *Policing Communities: Understanding Crime and Solving Problems*:

- *The New Police Order: Effectiveness, Equity, and Efficiency in Community Policing* (Eck and Rosenbaum)
- *The Changing Role of the Police: Assessing the Current Transition to Community Policing* (Rosenbaum)
- *Building a Responsive Community* (Gardner)
- *Social Capital and a Sense of Community Building: Building Social Cohesion* (Correia)
- *Community-Oriented Policing Across the U.S.: Facilitators and Impediments to Implementation* (Zhao, Thurman, & Lovrich)
- *Implementing Change: Community-Oriented Policing and Problem Solving* (Glensor & Peak)
- *Winning the Hearts and Minds of Police Officers: An Assessment of Staff Perceptions of Community Policing and Problem Solving* (Lurgio & Skogan)
- *Toward a Practical Approach to Organizational Change: Community Policing Initiatives in Six Cities* (Weisel & Eck)
- *The Current State and Future of Community Policing* (Tafoya)

Obviously, many of these titles are caught up in the "community policing" fervor, to be discussed below, but not all of them. Community policing itself was a result, not a cause, of the focus on community proceding the events of the 1960s. And so, while this relationship with the community remains filled with historical "baggage" and cannot in any way be considered "fixed" or "repaired," it has, at the very least, *changed*. The question that remains to be answered is, *in what ways*? I suggest that policing and community relationships have changed in at least three fundamental ways: in terms of collaborations, communication, and police isolation.

First, in terms of collaboration, crime control strategies in general have shifted to being community-based. With foot patrol and station houses, this was the traditional milieu of the "beat cop." The patrol car changed all this. As we have seen elsewhere in these pages, under the patrol car and the professional model, the police began seeing the layout of cities not in terms of neighborhoods, but in terms of beats and precincts, which may or may not coincide with community-defined areas. After the disastrous consequences of this disconnect from society was recognized, police slowly moved to conceptualizing their city differently, namely, in terms of organic and "natural" communities. Although difficult to define empirically, the very idea of community is so important to Americans as to allow researchers and police alike to work with community members (Thurman, Zhao, & Giacomazzi, 2001). These collaborations have adopted a number of guises, including community oriented policing. But there have been others. For example, Walker & Katz (2011) lists six community-based strategies that inhere working with neighborhood members: not relying on any single policy or practice; focusing on that area and on specific crimes or a specific crime in that area; engaging in problem-solving activities; partnering with community groups and other agencies; looking for non-criminal law sanctions/remedies; and relying on evidence-based solutions. As shall be seen below, these changes have been successfully implemented in a number of strategies, not just community policing.

Second, in terms of communication, the police have broadened their general communication strategies. Not only do the police work closely with news reporters, which they have always done, but they now use the Internet like never before. Some typical ways that the police use the Internet to better communicate with civilians include social media outlets, like Facebook, Twitter, and YouTube, and also their own web pages. Police department web pages often include real-time crime statistics, including crime maps, and the ability to file criminal complaints, pay fines, and offer both commendations and complaints against individual officers. Cell phones have also improved communication between civilians and police. It is almost standard procedure for police officers to hand out their cell phone numbers to concerned citizens, for example, after responding to a call for service.

Obviously, all of this has served to reduce the amount of isolation police feel in society, our third way in which the police have changed vis-a-vis the community. With the reduced sense of isolation has come a reduction in the "us versus them" attitude so endemic during the decades of the professional era. There still remain communication problems and the police remain committed to their brothers in blue, often feeling isolated by the actions of lawyers, the press, and community groups. Nevertheless, civilians are allowed "in" on everyday police operations more now than they were previously. It has done much to improve the rapport of police departments with minority communities. Although there is variation based on race, with more Blacks and Latinos disliking, distrusting, or thinking that the police do a poor job when compared to their White counterparts (cf. Walker, Spohn, & DeLone, 2011), it remains true that the majority of Americans, *net of race and net of class*, *like* the police. The police are trusted as being the most honest professionals in the United States, with only nurses, doctors, and high school teachers being ranked as more trustworthy (Walker & Katz, 2011). Scholars (e.g., Walker & Katz, 2011) agree that findings such as these are the result of improved use of force policies, better handling of citizen complaints, and an all around "paradigm shift" in how police view civilians. So even in this most volatile of domains, the police *have* improved considerably since the 1970s.

WHAT HAS *NOT* CHANGED

Although much has changed in policing since these three decades, much also remains the same. If someone from the 1950s were to travel into the 21st century, they would have no problem pointing out who the police were merely by their uniform or patrol cars. The bureaucratic nature of the professional policing model almost ensures the endurance of at least some of its characteristics. Indeed, the bureaucratic structure of police agencies has largely remained unchanged since the 1960s. Similarly, patrol remains relatively consonant: random and a hallmark of American police "services." Motorized patrol has itself secured the centralized nature of municipal policing, even while policing nationwide remains very decentralized (Mastrofski & Willis, 2010). This is due, no doubt, to American federalism. Yet it is also true that police departments behave similarly to one another, in both form and function, more so than they ever have before thanks to federal intervention and monies (Cooper, 2014).

The most accurate way to describe changes in policing across the nation since the 1970s would be in this unsatisfying word: *variable*. While it is true that police are more similar now than ever before, that does not mean that they are not different. Instead, even a cursory survey of American law enforcement reveals incredible variation in terms of what changes have been adopted—and where. This pattern (or lack thereof) is further complicated by the incredible ability of police agencies to absorb changes without changing their structure or even their typical operations (Mastrofski & Willis, 2010). It may even be accurate to suggest that American police departments, like their British counterparts (Brodgen & Ellison, 2013), are engaging in a form of change better characterized by consolidation and "belt-tightening," given the current status of government austerity. Whatever the case, the statements, *policing has changed considerably*, and *policing has not changed considerably*, are both simultaneously true in more than a Schrodingerian sense.

One specific area that requires some more detailed attention is in the realm of *community*. Above I have argued that, along with technology, we have seen the most important changes with the police in terms of their relationship with the community. This begs a very important question: why, then, has community policing not caught on to any appreciable degree? Such a question, for policing scholars, is unfortunately rife with misunderstandings and controversy. To clarify: community policing grew out the events of the 1950s, 1960s, and 1970s (Angell, 1971), and was first given coherent articulation from Trojanowicz and Bucqueroux (1990). Scholars continued to write about the utility and potential of community policing, giving special attention to the role of organizational change in making what amounts to a paradigm shift in the police mandate a reality (Cordner, 1999). Yet to date, there is no evidence that community policing has been adopted wholesale among police agencies (with the Chicago Police Department standing out as a possible exception—yet even this change began in 1993 and continues to be redefined today—see Chicago PD's website called "CLEARpath"). In other words, it is difficult to assess whether community policing "works" because it is difficult to pinpoint its adoption. Scholars are left evaluating community policing piecemeal, such as focusing on foot patrol or community meetings (Alpert & Moore, 1993; Greene & Taylor, 1988).

Yet we saw in chapter 2, policing has undergone paradigmatic shifts, specifically from the political to the professional eras. Why, then, were Vollmer and others able to institute change, yet the scholars of the late 1900s could not? This is a question with a complex answer. Part of the answer may be the following: Vollmer and others carved out a police mandate that earned legitimacy among the body politic; community oriented policing did not try to fit within this traditional mandate. Indeed, it attempted to replace the mandate of professional crime fighter with co-producer of justice with the community (Zhao, Thurman, & Lovrich, 1997). Other policing innovations that were tried around the same time as community policing, such as zero-tolerance or problem-oriented policing and COMPSTAT, maintained the role of police as expert, and have flourished and continue to flourish (Walker & Katz, 2011).

The implementation of community oriented policing is often held up as a poster-child for the difficulties inherent in organizational and behavioral change in police agencies. Even before Trojanowicz and Bucqueroux (1990) first fully articulated the idea of community policing as both a basic shift in policing form, function, and philosophy, such barriers were readily apparent in American policing. To wit, O.W. Wilson, policing reformer August Vollmer's protégé, though successful in reducing corruption among police officers in Wichita City, Kansas, was ultimately forced to resign as chief because of powerful political actors who did not appreciate his efforts. While this stands as an example of the resistance that efforts of change meet in the policing world, Wilson's failure to successfully adjust policing practices in the face of a racial crisis in Chicago during the 1960s reflects the police agency's dilatoriness in innovatively responding to environmental changes (Walker, 1998). A concern with community responsiveness and well-being has and continues to be at the core of the police mandate. As such, it has demanded the attention of scholars for decades (Reiss, 1971; Reisig, 2010). Such a concern, however, is couched within the traditional definition of "what the police do" (Zhao & Thurman, 1997). Despite federal monies

(Zhao, Scheider, & Thurman, 2002), community policing remains a "tool" rather than the paradigmatic overhaul it was intended to be (Maguire, 1997; Zhao, Lovrich, & Robinson, 2001).

But is the relationship between the police and minorities better—that is, has anything changed? Above, I have suggested a very qualified *yes*. It is worth digressing at this point with one such qualification. Despite strides in improving the relationship between the police and civilians, tensions do boil over into violence. The case of Ferguson, Missouri, stands as a stark example of this reality. In the middle of 2014, a white police officer shot a young black man in the St. Louis suburb of Ferguson; the outcry was swift and long. Riots, demonstrations, arrests, and violence attracted the attention of several stakeholders, including the media, the county, state, and federal govern-ments, and concerned faith-based groups. Even after several autopsies exon-erated the white officer, the tension was not attenuated by any appreciable degree. This was because the issue of race and the police was bigger than the officer and the young black male. Rather, they were a representation of all that had occurred before between the police and minority communities, and a palpable realization that there remains a long way to go before repairing over two hundred years of damaged relations between these two groups.

THE FUTURE OF POLICING

Two specific criminal justice approaches to crime control represent, in my opinion and that of other policing scholars (see citations throughout), the culmination of changes in policing *now* because of events *then*: Project Safe Neighborhoods (PSN) and the Smart Policing Initiative (SPI). Both of these capture all of the changes described above while preserving the unique role of police in American society: A focus on communities, on crime prevention, on interagency collaboration and communication, on the use of technology in policing and crime prevention, and on an expanded repertoire of crime fight-ing tools that include *non*-law enforcement options. Additionally, each are based in the "evidenced-based" or "what works" paradigm, but expand the paradigm considerably so that the discussion is not just about "getting things done." Instead, the discussion involves serious questions about the role of police in American society vis-a-vis crime, neighborhoods, and the Rule of Law in a way that has never been done. Previously, each of these domains were discussed separately, as if they had no impact one on the other. Both PSN and SPI recognize that crime, neighborhoods, and the Rule of Law, in the context of the police and crime control more broadly, have an interplay that is at once nuanced and impactful on all levels of society and on the profession of policing. Because of this nuanced relationship, both PSN and SPI consider the policing role not as if in a vacuum, but only in the broader socio-political context in a way that was completely lost on the professional policing model of the 1950s, 1960s, and 1970s. And by all academic accounts, so far, both models can safely, if with the typically qualified tone of voice so characteristic of academe, be considered to "work."

Project Safe Neighborhoods

The programmatic underpinnings and development of PSN is nowhere described better than in Klofas, Hipple, and McGarrell's (2010) monumentally important volume, *The New Criminal Justice: American Communities and the Changing World of Crime Control.* As the editors describe it, PSN did not develop out of the blue; rather, it was an improved iteration of a previous project run in both Richmond, Virginia and Rochester, New York called Project Exile. Aimed at gun violence, Project Exile featured federal prosecutors working closely with county prosecutors to ensure that convicted offenders received the harshest punishment possible. That is, if federal statute produced the harsher punishment, the federal government would prosecute the case; otherwise, the local prosecutors would. Project Exile not only involved regular interactions between federal and local prosecutors, but it also included a media blitz warning offenders of the new paradigm. Project Exile caught the attention of the federal government, which turned it into a full blown federal crime control program called Strategic Approach to Community Safety Initiative (SACSI). Like its predecessor, SACSI (which was housed under the National Institute of Justice) was prosecutor-based, with an emphasis on what would later be termed "pulling levers," a phrase which would come to mean no leniency, no plea bargaining, and no holds barred prosecution. Under the George W. Bush administration, SACSI would be turned into the broader PSN. Although PSN would be broader in application, it would maintain two important elements from Project Exile and SACSI: a focus on violent crime, particularly gun crime, and collaborative partnerships between criminal justice agencies. This latter element would expand greatly to include a host of other organizations and institutions, and with it, a host of non-law enforcement solutions to crime problems.

McGarrell (2010) breaks the PSN approach down into the following characteristics: strategic planning in collaboration with multiple partners, across agencies and non-law enforcement organizations; outreach to community members; data-based accountability mechanisms; and training, both for criminal justice actors and community members. In a sense, then, PSN is an operational approach to what DiIulio (1993) once described as the co-production of justice between citizens and law enforcement. McGarrell (2010) further notes that PSN can best be understood as encompassing three "core" themes: focusing resources on specific crimes and specific locations; data and research driven solutions; and expanding the boundaries of involvement in terms of justice production, crime control, and order maintenance. PSN is not only data-based, it is also theory-based. For example, much of contemporary law enforcement explicitly borrows from Cohen and Felson's (1979) Routine Activities Theory and from the more general theoretical framework of Situational Crime Prevention (Mock, 2010; Clarke, 1983). The connection between crime control and these rational theories should be intuitive—but as will be seen, sometimes the theoretical connection underpinning the behavior of PSN are not so obvious, but no less effective. In any case, the research aspect of PSN has been described as "action research," which can perhaps be understood as research that is embedded from start to finish in the crime control effort (Frabutt, Gathings, Harvey, & Di Luca, 2010; Greene, 2010). Although such research is not without its challenges, the pattern thus far with PSN is that these challenges can be overcome—and to great effect.

The flagship example of PSN is Boston's Operation Ceasefire (OC). As with its SACSI and Project Exile predecessors, and as its name implies, OC was born in response to gun violence and homicides. It focused solely on these crimes and in specific neighborhoods, and involved numerous agencies and community groups in a problem-oriented policing exercise. These groups included not just the police, probation/parole, and prosecutors, but also neighborhood leaders, such as Alcoholics Anonymous and clergy. While it employed the same pulling levers strategy used under Project Exile and SACSI, it also strived to improve the relationships between law enforcement and community members. This latter part was an innovation of OC that was based not on Routine Activities Theory or Situational Crime Prevention, but on Robert Sampson's influential collective efficacy interpretation of Social Disorganization Theory. Indeed, in a video available on YouTube (OJP, 2012), then Boston Police Commisioner Edward Davis cited Sampson and collective efficacy by name as being central to OC's success. Also in that video, Davis noted that OC would not have been effective were it not for the inclusion of Anthony Braga—a well-known policing scholar from Rutgers and Harvard. By almost all accounts, OC was a success at reducing both homicides and gun violence in Boston. But, as should be clear, doing so required not a "quick fix" but a concerted effort on the part of multiple parties, informed practices with a built in assessment, and a vision that reached beyond the immediate need of reducing crime. OC is not alone in demonstrating that, when done correctly, PSN can "work," as several contributing authors in *The New Criminal Justice* demonstrate. Clearly, policing *has* changed in its approach to communities, crime, and research.

Smart Policing Initiative

SPI stands for Smart Policing Initiative. The word *Smart* in SPI is itself an acronym: *specialized multi-agency response team*. It is directed by the Bu-

reau of Justice Assistance (BJA). Its website (http://www.
smartpolicinginitiative.com/) lays out the blueprint the SPI is built around:
"Building evidenced-based, data-driven law enforcement tactics and strategies that are effective, efficient, and economical." At the risk of simplifying
matters, SPI is based on the SARA model of POP, relies heavily on technology, and requires a "conscious effort" among all parties involved to collaborate toward the goal of crime prevention and reduction (Joyce, Ramsey, &
Stewart, 2013, p. 358). In this regard, the BJA puts its money where its
mouth is: it is a "consortium" (cf. its website) of researchers (both academic
and government) and local law enforcement agents, who work with other
stakeholders in the community. It is a natural outgrowth of PSN, and indicative of the popularization of POP. So it is not surprising that the Boston
Police were involved in SPI early on with their Safe Street Teams, which
focused on the reduction of crime in specific "hot spots" (Braga and Schnell,
2013).

SPI shares many characteristics with PSN. It is unique, however, in that it
finds its impetus directly with the police themselves, whereas PSN is often
directed from the prosecutor's office. Coldren, Huntoon, and Medaris (2013)
delineate the following general characteristics of SPI agencies:

- A focus on crime reduction, rather than crime fighting
- A commitment to evidenced-based practices
- A realignment of the goals of police such that they become operational—
  that is, measurable and realistic. (It may not be coincidental that SMART
  policing shares an acronym with SMART goals.)
- Improving not only effectiveness, but efficiency
- To encourage innovation in crime reduction that includes non-law-en-
  forcement solutions

The importance, direction, and current evaluative status of SPI were highlighted recently in a special issue of the PERF subsidized, peer reviewed
journal *Police Quarterly*. Two articles in particular explored the current effectiveness of SPI. First, that by White and Katz (2013), who described and
evaluated the cleverly titled "Operation Not-So-Convenient." Working with
researchers from Arizona State University's Center for Violence Prevention
and Community Safety, Glendale police officers used the SARA model to
come up with several solutions to the ongoing problem of gas-station robberies. Their solutions included both law enforcement practices (traditional sup-
pression techniques) and non-law enforcement practices, in this case training
convenience store owners in CPTED practices. White and Katz's evaluation
suggested a 49 percent reduction in gas station robberies that were part of the
project, compared to a null difference among non-targeted gas stations. Second, Uchida and Swatt (2013) evaluated Los Angeles' Strategic Extraction

and Restoration Program, aka Operational LASER. This SPI project was aimed at reducing gun violence by focusing on chronic *offenders* and chronic *locations* (characterized by high volumes of gun crime), via directed patrol, focused bike patrol, and the use of CCTV's. Uchida and Swatt's factorial model included chronic offender only, chronic location only, and chronic offender and location interaction models. They ultimately found that *only* those strategies aimed at *both* offenders and locations saw a significant reduction in gun violence. All of this was done in collaboration with researchers, key community stakeholders, and other criminal justice actors.

CONCLUSIONS

It is too soon to determine that either PSN *or* SPI are *the* new models of law enforcement, but they are certainly representative of where policing is going. Additionally, they are the culmination of three decades of policing missteps: poor community relations, reactive techniques, a lack of assessment, and a culture of isolation. Still, not everything has changed. The policing mandate, for one, remains focused on professional crime fighting, while at the same time being "a hodge-podge of conflicting duties and responsibilities" (White, 2007, p. 205). And relations between the police and minority communities are still strained—as Ferguson attests to. Indeed, a recent poll from the Pew Research Forum (2014) still indicates a sharp divide in public opinion vis-a-vis the police in terms of holding officers accountable, treating people of different racial ethnic groups equally, use of force, respecting privacy, and even protecting people from crime. Although most people have confidence in the police, minorities continue to have less confidence than their white counterparts.

Still, there is reason to hope that we are not returning to the policing of the 1950s, 1960s, and 1970s, Ferguson notwithstanding. With the introduction and institutionalization of both PSN and SPI, in tandem with new measures of goal achievement that include citizen opinions about the police, police are finding a mean between preventing and reducing crime and working with the public as co-producers of justice (DiIulio, 1993) in a way that works. Perhaps the most important evidence of this new era in policing, at least in terms of public/policing relations, was what has been labeled "The Apology Heard Around the World" (StoryofAmerica, 2013), where in 2013 then Montgomery, Alabama police chief Kevin Murphy apologized to United States Representative John Lewis for the part that the police played during the 1960s *against* the Freedom Riders at the height of the Civil Rights Movement. Lewis was among those who were beaten by Montgomery police in the summer of 1961. What is striking about this is that Murphy was willing to take responsibility for the actions of his predecessors. As much as this book has focused on *the police*, the fact of the matter is that crime is a *societal* issue, and any significant changes in crime—and in the relation between police and minority communities—can only be made at that level. This must, of necessity, include all of society, not just the police, taking responsibility for what has gone on before, and taking an active role in how we will proceed into the future.

References

Alpert, G. P., & Moore, M .H. (1993). Measuring police performance in the new paradigm of policing. In J. J. DiIulio and others, *Performance measures for the criminal justice system.* NCJ-143505. Washington, DC: U.S. Department of Justice, Bureau of Justice Statistics.

Angell, J. E. (1971). Toward an alternative to the classic police organizational arrangements: A democratic model. *Criminology, 9*(2-3), 185–206.

Banton, M. (1964). *The policeman in the community.* London: Tavistock Publications.

Barker, T. (1977). Peer group support for police occupational deviance. *Criminology, 15,* 353–66.

Bayley, D. & Mendelsohn, H. (1969). *Minorities and the police.* New York: Free Press.

Beccaria, C. (1764; 1995). *On crimes and punishment and other writing.* New York: Cambridge University Press.

Bentham, J. (1789; 1961). An introduction to the principles of moral and legislation. In *Utilitarianism* (pp. 7–398). Garden City, NY: Doubleday.

Bernard, T. J., & Engel, R. S. (2001). Conceptualizing criminal justice theory. *Justice Quarterly, 18,* 1–30.

Bittner, E. (1967). "The police on skid-row. A study of peace keeping." In *Criminal Justice process—A Reader*, eds. W.B. Sanders and H.C. Daudistel. New York: Praeger.

Bittner, E. (1970). *The function of the police in modern society: A review of background factors, current practices and possible role models.* National Institute of Mental Health, Center for Studies of Crime and Delinquency, Bethesda, Maryland.

Black, D. (1976). *The behavior of law.* New York: Academic Press.

Black, D. (1979). Common sense in the sociology of law. *American Sociological Review, 44*(1), 18–27.

Black, D., & Reiss, A. J. (1970). Police control of juveniles. *American Sociological Review, 35* 63–77.

Blumstein, A. (2006). Disaggregating the violence trends. In Blumstein, A., & Wallman, J. (Eds.). *The crime drop in America* (Revised ed.) (pp. 13–44). New York: Cambridge University Press

Blumstein, A., & Wallman, J.(Eds.). (2006). *The crime drop in America* (Revised ed.). New York: Cambridge University Press.

Bopp, W. J. (1977). OW Wilson and the Search for a Police Profession. *Port Washington, NY: National University Publications.*

Bordua, D. J. (1967). *The police: Six sociological essays.* New York: John Wiley & Sons.

Bordua, D., & Tifft, L. (1971). Citizen interviews, organizational feedback, and police-community relations decisions. *Law & Society Review. 6*(2), 155–183.

Bostaph, L. G., & Cooper, J. A. (2007). "History of the victims' rights movement" in Lisa Growette Bostaph & Jonathon Cooper (Eds.), *Idaho Victims Assistance Manual.*

Braga, A. A., & Schnell, C. (2013). Evaluating place-based policing strategies: Lessons learned from the smart policing initiative in Boston. *Police Quarterly, 16*, 338–357.

Brogden, M., & Ellison, G. (2013). *Policing in an age of austerity: A postcolonial perspective.* New York: Routledge.

Brooks, L. W. (2005). Police discretionary behavior: A study of style. In R. Durham and G. Alpert (Eds.) *Critical issues in policing* (122-142). Illinois: Waveland Press.

Brown, M. (1981). *Working the street: Police discretion and the dilemmas of reform.* New York: Russell Sage.

Burke, L. (2011). Revolution or evolution? *Probation Journal, 58*(1), 3–8.

Buysse, V., & Wesley, P. W. (2006). Evidence-based practice: How did it emerge and what does it really mean for the early childhood field? *Zero to Three Journal, 27*(2), 50–55.

Cahn, M., & Tien, J. M. (1981). *An evaluation report of an alternative approach in police response: The Wilmington Management of Demand Program.* Cambridge, MA: Public Systems Evaluation, Inc.

Chambliss, W. (1971). Vice, corruption, bureaucracy and power. *Wisconsin Law Review, 4*, 1150–73.

Chappell, A. T., & Piquero, A. R. (2004). Applying social learning theory to police misconduct. *Deviant Behavior, 25*, 85–208.

Clarke, R. (1983). Situational crime prevention: Its theoretical basis and practical scope. *Crime and Justice, 4*, 225–256.

Cohen, L. E., & Felson, M. (1979). Social change and crime rate trends: A routine activity approach. *American Sociological Review, 44*(4), 588–608.

Coldren, J. R., Huntoon, A., & Medaris, M. (2013). Introducing smart policing: Foundations, principles, and practice. *Police Quarterly, 16*, 275–286.

Cooper, J. A. (2010). Noble cause corruption as a consequence of role conflict in the police organization. *Policing and Society: An International Journal of Research and Policy, 22*, 169-184.

Cooper, J. A. (2010). Police unionism and collective bargaining. *Police Forum, 19*(1), 1–14.

Cooper, J. A., & Bolen (2013). Without regard to the usual rules. In Peter A. Collins & David C. Brody (Eds.) *Crime & Justice in the City: As Seen through* The Wire. Durham, NC: Carolina Academic Press.

Cooper, J. A. (2014). *In search of police legitimacy: Territoriality, isomorphism, and changes in policing practices.* El Paso, TX: LFB Scholarly Publishing LLC.

Cooper, J. A., White, M. D., Ward, K. C., Raganella, A. J., & Saunders, J. (2014). Exploring the nexus of officer race/ethnicity, sex, and job satisfaction: The case of the NYPD. *Criminology, Criminal Justice Law & Society 15*(2) 43–59.

Cooper, J. A., & Worrall, L. (2012). Theorizing criminal justice evaluation and research. *Criminal Justice Review, 37*, 384–397.

Cordner, G. W. (1999). The elements of community policing. In L. Gaines and G. W. Cordner (Eds.), *Policing perspectives: An anthology* (pp. 137–149). Los Angeles, CA: Roxbury.

Corsianos, M. (2003). Discretion in detectives' decision making and 'high profile' cases. *Police Practice and Research: An International Journal, 4*(3), 301–314.

Crank, J. P., & Caldero, M. A. (2000). *Police ethics: The corruption of noble cause.* Cincinnati, OH: Anderson Publishing Co.

Crank, J. P. (2003). Institutional theory of police: A review of the state of the art. *Policing: An International Journal of Police Strategies & Management, 26*, 186–207.

Crank, J. P. (2004). *Understanding police culture* (2nd ed.). Cincinnati, OH: Anderson.

Cullen, F. T., Wright, J. P., & Blevins, K. R. (2009). *Taking stock: The status of criminological theory.* New Brunswick, NJ: Transaction Publishers.

Dawson, R. O. (1969). *Sentencing: The decision as to type, length, and conditions of sentence.* Chicago: Little, Brown.

Decker, S. E. (2010). Forward. In Klofas, J., Hipple, N. K., & McGarrell, E. (Eds.). *The new criminal justice: American communities and the changing world of crime control* (pp. xi-xiv). New York: Routledge.

Delattre. E. J. (2006). *Characters and Cops*. Washington, DC. AEI Press

DiIulio, J. J. (1993). Measuring performance when there is no bottom line. In J. J. DiIulio (Ed.), *Performance Measures for the Criminal Justice System* (pp. 147–160). Washington, DC: U.S. Government Printing Office.

Durkheim, E. ([1997]; 1933). *The Division of Labor in Society*. Glencoe, IL: Free Press.

Duffin, A. T. (2010). *History in Blue: 160 Years of Women Police, Sheriffs, Detectives, and State Troopers*. New York: Kaplan Publishing.

Eisenstein, J., & Jacob, H. (1977). *Felony Justice*. Boston: Little, Brown and Co.

Ford, M. (Director). *Uprising: Hip Hop & The LA Riots* (2012). In W. Jones (Producer). *VH1 Rock*.

Fosdick, R. (1969). *American police systems*. Montclair, NJ: Paterson-Smith.

Fox, J. A. (2006). Demographics and U.S. Homicide. In Blumstein, A., & Wallman, J. (Eds.), *The crime drop in America* (Revised ed.) (pp. 288–318). New York: Cambridge University Press.

Frabutt, J. M., Gathings, M. J., Harvey, L. K., & Di Luca, K. (2010). Added value through a partnership model of action research: A case example from a Project Safe Neighborhoods Research Partner. In J. M. Klofas, N. K. Hipple, & E. F. McGarrell (Eds), *The new criminal justice: American communities and the changing world of crime control* (pp. 103–113). New York: Routledge.

Furstenberg, F. J., & Wellford, C. F. (1973). Calling the police: The evaluation of public service. *Law and Society Review, 7*, 393–406.

Fyfe, J. J. (1979). Administrative interventions on police shooting discretion: An empirical examination. *Journal of Criminal Justice, 7*, 309–324.

Fyfe, J. J. (1982). Blind justice: Police shootings in Memphis. *Journal of Criminal Law and Criminology, 73*, 707-722.

Fyfe, J. J. (1983). Enforcement Workshop: The NIJ Study of the Exclusionary Rule. *Criminal Law Bulletin, 19*(3), 253–260.

Fyfe, J. J. (1986). The split-second syndrome and other determinants of police violence. In *Violent Transactions*. (eds.) Campbell, A. & Gibbs, J.J. Oxford: Basil Blackwell.

Fyfe, J. J. (1988). Police use of deadly force: Research and reform. *Justice Quarterly, 5*(2), 165–201.

Glensor, R. W., Correia, M. E., & Peak, K. J. (2000). *Policing communities: Understanding crime and solving problems*. Los Angeles, CA: Roxbury.

Goffman, E. (1961). *Asylums: Essays on the social situations of mental patients and other inmates*. New York: Anchor Books.

Goldstein, H. (1977). *Policing a free society*. Cambridge, MA: Ballinger.

Goldstein, H. (1979). Improving policing: A problem-oriented approach. *Crime and Delinquency, 25*: 236–258.

Goldstein, H. (1990). *Excellence in problem-oriented policing*. New York: McGraw-Hill.

Goldstein, J. (1960). Police discretion not to invoke the criminal process: Low-visibility decisions in the administration of justice. *Yale Law Journal, 69*, 643-594.

Gottfredson, M. R., & Gottfredson, D. M. (1988). *Decision making in criminal justice: Toward the rational exercise of discretion*. 2nd ed. *Law, Society, and Policy*, Vol 3. New York: Plenum Press.

Gottfredson, M., & Hirschi, T. (1990). *A general theory of crime*. California: Stanford University Press.

Graham, F. P. (1970). *The Due Process Revolution: the Warren Court's impact on criminal law*. Alpharetta, GA: Hayden Book Company.

Greene, J. A. (1999). Zero tolerance: A case study of police policies and practices in New York City. *Crime & Delinquency, 45*, 171-187.

Greene, J. R. (2010). Collaborations between police and academic/research organizations: Some prescriptions from the field. In J. M. Klofas, N. K. Hipple, & E. F. McGarrell (Eds). *The new criminal justice: American communities and the changing world of crime control* (pp. 121–127). New York: Routledge.

Greene, J. R. (2013). New directions in policing: Balancing prediction and meaning in police research. *Justice Quarterly, 31*, 193–228.

148   *References*

Greene, J. R., & Taylor, R. B. (1988). Communtiy policing and foot patrol: Issues of theory and evaluation. In J. R. Greene & S. Mastrofski (eds.), *Communtiy policing: Rhetoric or reality.* New York: Praeger.

Greenwood, P. W., & Petersilia, J. (1975). *The criminal investigation process.* Santa Monica, CA: Rand Corporation.

Hall, P. G., & Hay, D. (1980). *Growth centres in the European urban system.* Oakland, CA: University of California Press.

Harris, D. A. (2002). *Profiles in injustice: Why police profiling cannot work.* New York: The New Press.

Hayde, M. J. (2001). *My Name's Friday: The Unauthorized But True Story of Dragnet and the Films of Jack Webb.* Nashville, TN: Cumberland House Publishing.

Hemmens, C., Worrall, J. L., & Thompson, A. (2004). *Significant Cases in Criminal Procedure.* Criminal Justice Case Briefs series. Los Angeles, CA: Roxbury Publishing Company.

Herbert, S. (2001). Policing the contemporary city: Fixing broken windows or shoring up neoliberalism? *Theoretical Criminology, 5*(4), 445–466.

Hopkins, E. (1931). *Our lawless police.* New York: Wiley.

Horwitz, M. J. (1998). *The Warren court and the pursuit of justice.* New York: Hill and Wang.

Institute for the Study of Labor and Economic Crisis (1982). *The iron fist and the velvet glove: An analysis of U.S. police.* In V.E. Kappeler (Ed.) *The police and society: Touchstone readings.* Long Grove, IL: Waveland Press, Inc.

Ivkovic, S. K. (2005). Police misbehavior: A cross-cultural study of corruption seriousness. *Policing: An International Journal of Police Strategies & Management, 28*(3) 546–566.

Jackson, P. (1989). *Minority group threat, crime, and policing.* New York: Praeger.

Jacob, H. (1971). Black and White perceptions of justice in the city. *Law and Society Review, 6*, 69–90.

Johnson, D. R. (1981). *American law enforcement—A history.* Missouri: Forum Press.

Johnson, L. B. (1965). *State of the Union Address: Lyndon B. Johnson.* Hazelton, PA: The Electronic Classics Series.

Joyce, N. M., Ramsey, C. H., & Stewart, J. K. (2013). Commentary on smart policing. *Police Quarterly, 16*, 358–368.

Kane, R. J. (2002). The social ecology of police misconduct. *Criminology, 40*, 867–896.

Kane, R. J. (2005). Compromised police legitimacy as a predictor of violent crime in structurally disadvantaged communities. *Criminology, 43*(2), 469–498.

Kappeler, V. E., Sluder, V. E., & Alpert, G. P. (1998). *Forces of deviance: understanding the dark side of policing.* 2nd ed. Prospect Heights, IL: Waveland Press

Kelling, G. L., & Coles, C. M. (1998). *Fixing broken windows: Restoring order in american cities.* New York: Martin Kessler Books/Free Press.

Kelling, G. L., & Moore, M. H. (1988). *The evolving strategy of policing.* Washington, DC: US Department of Justice, Office of Justice Programs, National Institute of Justice.

Kelling, G. L., Pate, A. M., Dieckman, D., & Brown, C. (1974). *The Kansas City preventive patrol experiment: Technical report.* Washington, DC: Police Foundation.

Kelling, G. L., & Wilson, J. Q. (1982). Broken windows: The police and neighborhood safety. *Atlantic Monthly, 249*(3), 29–38.

Klinger, D. A. (1997). Negotiating order in patrol work: An ecological theory of police response to deviance. *Criminology, 35*(2), 277–306.

Klockars, C. B. (1980). The *Dirty Harry* problem. *The Annals of the American Academy of Political and Social Science, 452*, 33-47.

Klockars, C. B. (1986). Street justice: Some micro-moral reservations: Comment on Sykes. *Justice Quarterly, 3*, 513-516.

Klofas, J., Hipple, N. K., & McGarrell, E. (2010). *The new criminal justice: American communities and the changing world of crime control.* New York: Routledge.

Kraska, P. (2003). *Theorizing criminal justice: Eight essential orientations.* Long Grove, IL.: Waveland Press, Inc.

Kraska, P. B. (2006). Criminal justice theory: Toward legitimacy and an infrastructure. *Justice Quarterly, 23*(02), 167–185.

LaFave, W. R. (1965). *Arrest: The decision to take a suspect into custody.* Boston: Little, Brown.

Lane, R. (1980). Urban police and crime in nineteenth-century America. *Crime and Justice, 2,* 1–43.

Langworthy, R. H. (1986). *The structure of police organizations.* New York: Praeger.

Laub, J. H. (2012). *John H. Laub: A culture of science—a message from the NIJ director.* Accessed online December 2014 via https://www.youtube.com/watch?v=34sQ-MgsVOQ

Leo, R. A. (1996). The impact of Miranda revisited. *Journal of Criminal Law and Criminology, 86,* 621-692.

Litwin, K. J. (2004). A multilevel multivariate analysis of factors affecting homicide clearance. *Journal of Research in Crime and Delinquency, 41,* 327-351.

Lumet, S. (Director), & Bregman, M. (Producer). (1973). *Serpico* [Biographical motion picture]. United States: Artists Entertainment Complex.

Lynch, J. P., & Addington, L. A. (Eds.). (2006). *Understanding crime statistics: Revisiting the divergence of the NCVS and the UCR.* New York: Cambridge University Press.

Maguire, E. R. (1997). Structural changes in large municipal police organizations during the community policing era. *Justice Quarterly, 14,* 547–576.

Manning, P. K. (1977). *Police work: The social organization of policing.* Cambridge, MA: MIT Press.

Manning, P. K. (1978). The police: Mandate, strategies, and appearances. In P. K. Manning and J. Van Maanen (Eds.), *Policing: A view from the street.* (7–31). Chicago, IL: Goodyear Publishing Company.

Manning, P. K. (1992). *Organizational communication.* New York: Aldine de Gruyter.

Martin, S. (1979). POLICEwomen and policeWOMEN: Occupation role dilemmas and choices of female offenders. *Journal of Police Science and Administration, 2*(3), 314–323.

Martinson, R. (1974). What works? Questions and answers about prison reform. *The Public Interest, 35*(2), 22–54.

Mastrofski, S. D., & Willis, J. J. (2010). Police organization continuity and change: Into the twenty-first century. In M. Toney (ed.). *Crime and justice: A review of research* (pp. 55–144). Oxford, UK: Oxford University Press.

McGarrell, E. F. (2010). Strategic problem solving, project safe neighborhoods, and the new criminal justice. In J. M. Klofas, N. K. Hipple, & E. F. McGarrell (Eds), *The new criminal justice: American communities and the changing world of crime control* (pp. 28–38). New York: Routledge.

McLaughlin, E. & Muncie, J. (Eds.; 2001). *Controlling crime.* London: Sage.

Miller, F. W. (1969). *Prosecution: The decision to charge a suspect with a crime.* Boston: Little, Brown.

Mock, L. F. (2010). Action research for crime control and prevention. In J. M. Klofas, N. K. Hipple, & E. F. McGarrell (Eds), *The new criminal justice: American communities and the changing world of crime control* (pp. 97–102). New York: Routledge.

Monkkonen, E. H. (1981). *Police in urban America 1860–1920.* New York: Cambridge University Press.

Morris, A. (1975). The American Society of Criminology: A history, 1941–1974. *Criminology,* 123–167.

Morrison, P. N., & Meyer, C. K. (1974). *A microanalysis of assaults on police in Austin, Texas.* Norman: Bureau of Government Research, University of Oklahoma.

Muir, W. K. (1977). *Police: Streetcorner politicians.* Chicago, IL: University of Chicago Press.

National Research Council. (2004). *Fairness and Effectiveness in Policing: The Evidence.* Skogan, W., & Kathleen Frydl. Committee to Review Research on Police Policy and Practices and Committee on Law and Justice. Division of Behavioral and Social Sciences Education. Washington, DC: National Academies Press.

Newman, D. J. (1966). *Conviction: The determination of guilt or innocence without trial.* Boston: Little, Brown.

Newton, J. (2006). *Justice for all: Earl Warren and the nation he made.* New York: Riverhead Books.

Niederhoffer, A. (1969). *Behind the Shield: The Police in Urban Society*. Garden City, NJ: Doubleday Publishing.

Omnibus Crime Control and Safe Streets Act. (1968). 42 U.S.C. 3789d.

OJP (2012). *Action research and the community to criminal justice feedback loop, Edward Davis.* Accessed online December 2014 via https://www.youtube.com/watch?v=uu4sSM0xOII&feature=youtu.be

Orfield Jr., M. W. (1987). The exclusionary rule and deterrence: An empirical study of Chicago narcotics officers. *The University of Chicago Law Review*, 1016–1069.

Packer, H. L. (1964). Two models of the criminal process. *University of Pennsylvania Law Review*, *13*(1), 1–68.

Packer, H. L. (1968). *The limits of the criminal sanction.* Palo Alto, CA: Stanford University Press.

Pate, T., Ferrara, A., Bowers, R. A., & Lorence, J. (1976). *Police response time: Its determinants and effects.* Washington, DC: Police Foundation.

Peel, R. (1829). Principles of Law Enforcement. The Metropolitan Police Act of 1829.

Pew Research Forum (2014). *Few say police forces nationally do well in treating races equally.* Accessed online November 2014, via http://www.people-press.org/2014/08/25/few-say-police-forces-nationally-do-well-in-treating-races-equally/

Platt, T. (1977). *The child savers: The invention of delinquency.* Chicago, IL: University of Chicago Press.

Polanyi, K. (2001). *The great transformation: The political and economic origins of our time.* Boston, MA: Beacon Press.

Pratt, T. C., Cullen, F. T., Blevins, K. R., Diagle, L. E., & Madensen, T. D. (2006). The empirical status of deterrence theory: A meta-analysis. In F. T. Cullen, J. Wright, & K. Blevins (Eds.), *Taking stock: The status of criminological theory*, 367–395. New Brunswick, NJ: Transaction Publishers.

President's Commission on Law Enforcement and Administration of Justice. (1967). *The Challenge of Crime in a Free Society.* US Government Printing Office.

President's Commission of Law Enforcement and Administration of Justice. (1967). *Task force report: Science and technology.* US Government Printing Office.

Reisig, M. D. (2010). Community and problem-oriented policing. *Crime and Justice: A Review of Research, 39*, 1–53.

Reiss, A. J. (1968). Sociology: The field. In *International Encyclopedia of the Social Sciences*, 1–22. New York: Macmillan/Free Press.

Reiss, A. J. (1971). *The police and the public.* New Haven: Yale University Press.

Reiss, A. J. (1992). Police organizations in the twentieth century. *Crime and Justice, 15,* 51–97.

Reppetto, T. (2010). *American police: A history, 1845–1945.* New York: Enigma Books.

Rice, S. K., & White, M. D. (Eds.). (2010). *Race, ethnicity, and policing: New and essential readings.* New York University Press.

Roberg, R., Novak, K., Cordner, G., & Smith, B. (2012). *Police & Society* (5th ed.). Oxford University Press.

Rojek, J., Rosenfeld, R., & Decker, S. (2012). Policing race: The racial stratification of searchers in police traffic stops. *Criminology, 50*(4), 993–1024.

Rosenfeld, R., Fornango, R., & Baumer, E. (2005). Did Ceasefire, CompStat, and Exile reduce homicide? *Criminolgy and Public Policy, 4*, 419–450.

Rosenfeld, R., Fornango, R., & Rengifo, A. F. (2007). The impact of order-maintenance on New York City homicide and robbery rates: 1988–2001. *Criminology, 45*(2), 355–384.

Rubinstein, J. (1973). *City police.* London: Macmillan.

Russell-Brown, K. (2009). *The color of crime: Racial hoaxes, white fear, black protectionism, police harassment, and other macroaggressions.* New York: NYU Press.

Schulhofer, S. (1998). Miranda's practical effect: Substantial benefits and vanishingly small social costs. In R. Leo & G. Thomas III (Eds.), *The Miranda debate: Law, justice, and policing* (pp. 191–207). Boston: Northeastern University Press.

Schwartz, W. F. (2002). Long-shot class actions. *Legal Theory, 8*(03), 297–311.

Sherman, L. W. (Ed.). (1974). *Police corruption: A sociological perspective.* Garden City, NY: Anchor Press.

Sherman, L. W. (1992). *Policing domestic violence: Experiments and dilemmas.* New York: Free Press.

Sherman, L. W. & Berk, R. A. (1984). The Minneapolis domestic violence experiment. *Police Foundation Reports.*

Sherman, L. W., & Weisburd, D. L. (1995). General deterrent effects of police patrol in crime "hot spots": A randomized, controlled trial. *Justice Quarterly, 12*, 625–648.

Silberman, C. E. (1978). *Criminal violence, criminal justice.* New York: Random House.

Sindall, K. & Sturgis, P. (2013). Austerity policing: Is visibility more important than absolute numbers in determining public confidence in the police? *European Journal of Criminology, 10*, 137–153.

Skogan, W. G. (2010). The challenge of timeliness and utility in research and evaluation. In J. Kolfas, N. Hipple & E. McGarrell (Eds.), *The new criminal justice: American communities and the changing world of crime control* (pp. 28–31). New York: Routledge.

Skolnick, J. H. (1966). *Justice without trial: Law enforcement in democratic society.* New York: John Wiley & Sons.

Skolnick, J. H. (1977). A sketch of the police officer's "working personality." In J. Goldsmith & S. Goldsmith (Eds.), *The police community* (pp. 101–122). Pacific Palisades, CA: Palisades.

Skolnick, J. H. (1982). Deception by police. *Criminal Justice Ethics*, 1(2).

Skolnick, J. H., & Fyfe, J. J. (1993). *Above the law: Police and the excessive use of force.* New York: Free Press.

Smith, D. A., Visher, C. A., & Davidson, L. A. (1984). Equity and discretionary justice: The influence of race on police arrest decisions. *Criminal Law & Criminology, 75.*

StoryofAmerica (2013). *Police chief's "apology heard around the world."* Accessed online December 2014, via http://youtu.be/vKBVtLn5T1k

Strecher, V. G. (1971). *The environment of law enforcement: A community relations guide.* Englewood cliffs, NJ: Prentice Hall.

Strecher, V. G. (1991). Histories and futures of policing: Readings and misreadings of a pivotal present. *Police Forum, 1*(1), 1–9.

Sykes, G. W. (1986). Street justice: A moral defense of order maintenance policing. *Justice Quarterly, 3*(4).

Thurman, Q. T., Zhao, J., & Giacomazzi, A. L. (2001). Community policing in a community era: An introduction and exploration. Los Angeles, CA: Roxbury.

Tiffany, L. P., McIntyre, D. M., & Rotenberg, D. (1967). *Detection of crime: Stopping and questioning, search and seizure, encouragement and entrapment.* Boston: Little, Brown.

Tonnies, F. (2002 [1957]). *Gemeinschaft und Gesellschaft.* New York: Harper & Row.

Trojanowicz, R., & Bucqueroux, B. (1990). *Community policing. A contemporary perspective.* Cincinnati, OH: Anderson Publishing Co.

Twersky-Glasner, A. (2005). Police personality: What is it and why are they like that? *Journal of Police and Criminal Psychology, 20*(1), 56–67.

Tyler, T. R. (2006). *Why people obey the law.* Princeton, NJ: Princeton University Press.

Uchida, C. D. (2005). The development of the American police. In R. Durham and G. Alpert (Eds.) *Critical issues in policing* (pp. 17–36). Illinois: Waveland Press.

Uchida, C. D. & Swatt, M. L. (2013). Operation LASER and the effectiveness of hotspot patrol: A panel analysis. *Police Quarterly, 16*, 287–304.

U.S. Riot Report (1968). *Report of the national advisory commission on civil disorders.* New York: Bantam Books.

Van Maanen, J. (1974). Working the street: A developmental view of police behavior. In H. Jacob (ed.), *The Potential for Reform of Criminal Justice* (Sage Criminal Justice System Annual Review, Vol. 3). Beverly Hills, CA: Sage Publication. 83–130.

Van Maanen, J. (1978). The asshole. In P. K. Manning and J. Van Maanen (Eds.), *Policing: A view from the street* (pp. 221–238). Chicago, IL: Goodyear Publishing Company.

Visher, C. A. (1983). Gender, police arrest decisions, and notions of chivalry. *Criminology, 21*, 5–28.

Wadman, R. C., & Allison, W. T. (2004). *To protect and to serve: A history of police in America.* Upper Saddle River, NJ: Pearson/Prentice Hall.

Walker, S. (1977). *A critical history of police reform.* Massachusetts: DC Heath and Company.

Walker, S. (1992). *Taming the system: The control of discretion in criminal justice, 1950–1990.* New York: Oxford University Press.

Walker, S. (1997). *The police in America: An introduction.* New York: McGraw Hill.

Walker, S. (1998). *Popular justice: A history of American criminal justice* (2nd ed.). New York: Oxford University Press.

Walker, S. (2005). *The new world of police accountability.* California: Sage Publications.

Walker, S. (2007). *Police accountability: Current issues and research needs.* Washington DC: National Institute of Justice.

Walker, S. (2011). *Sense and nonsense about crime, drugs, and communities: A policy guide* (7th ed.). Belmont, CA: Wadsworth, Cengage Learning.

Walker, S. (2015). *Sense and nonsense about crime, drugs, and communities: A policy guide* (8th ed.). Stamford, CT: Cengage Learning.

Walker, S., Alpert, G. P., & Kenney, D. J. (2001). Early warning systems: Responding to the problem police officer. Washington DC: National Institute of Justice, Research in Brief.

Walker, S., & Katz, C. M. (2011). *The police in America: An introduction.* New York: McGraw-Hill.

Walker, S., Spohn, C., & DeLone, M. (2012). *The color of justice: Race, ethnicity, and crime in America,* (5th ed.). California: Wadsworth.

Warner, B. D. (1997). Community characteristics and the recording of crime: Police recording of citizens' complaints of burglary and assault. *Justice Quarterly, 14,* 631-650.

Webb, J. (2005). *The Badge: True and Terrifying Crime Stories that Could Not be Presented on TV, from the Creator and Star of Dragnet.* New York, NY: Thunder's Mouth Press.

Weber, M. (2004). *The vocation lectures.* Indianapolis: Hackett Publishing Company.

Weitzer, R. (1999). Citizens' perceptions of police misconduct: Race and neighborhood context. *Justice Quarterly, 16*(4) 819–846.

Weitzer, R., & Tuch, S. A. (2004). Racially biased policing: Determinants of citizen perceptions. *Social Forces, 83*(3), 1009–1030.

Weitzer, R., Tuch, S. A., & Skogan, W. G. (2008). Police community relations in a majority-black city. *Journal of Research in Crime and Delinquency, 45,* 398–428.

Westley, W. A. (1970). *Violence and the Police: A Sociological Study of Law, Custom, and Morality.* Cambridge, MA: MIT Press.

White, M. D. (2007). *Current issues and controversies in policing.* Pearson Allyn and Bacon.

White, M. D. & Katz, C. M. (2013). Policing convenience store crime: Lessons from the Glendale, Arizona smart policing initiative. *Police Quarterly, 16,* 305–322.

William, M. & Snortum, J. (1984). Detective work: The criminal investigation process in a medium-size police department. *Criminal Justice Review, 9,* 33–39.

Williams, H., & Murphy, P. (1990). *The evolving strategy of police: A minority view.* U.S. Department of Justice, Office of Justice Programs, National Institute of Justice.

Wilson, J. Q. (1968). *Varieties of police behavior: The management of law and order in eight communities.* Cambridge, MA: Harvard University Press.

Wilson, O. (1963). *Police administration.* New York: McGraw-Hill.

Wolfe, S. E. & Piquero, A. R. (2011). Organizational justice and police misconduct. *Criminal Justice and Behavior, 38,* 332–353.

Worrall, J. L., & Zhao, J. (2003). The role of the COPS office in community policing. *Policing: An International Journal of Police Strategies & Management, 26*(1), 64–87.

Zehr, H. (2002). *The little book of restorative justice.* Intercourse, PA: Good Books.

Zhao, J. S., & Hassell, K. D. (2005). Policing styles and organizational priorities: Retesting Wilson's theory of local political culture. *Police Quarterly, 8,* 411–430.

Zhao, J. S., He, N., & Lovrich, N. P. (2003). Community policing: Did it change the basic functions of policing in the 1990s? A national follow-up study. *Justice Quarterly, 20*(4), 697–724.

Zhao, J. S., Thurrnan, Q. C. (1997). Facilitators and obstacles to community policing in a rural setting. In Q. Thurman, and E. McGarrell (eds.), *Community policing in a rural setting.* Cincinnati, OH: Anderson.

Zhao, J. S., Lovrich, N. P., & Robinson, T. H. (2001). Communtiy policing: Is it changing functions of policing? Findings from longitudinal study of 200+ municipal police agencies. *Journal of Criminal Justice, 29*, 365–377.

Zhao, J. S., Thurman, Q. T., & Lovrich, N. P. (1997). Community policing in the U.S.: Where are we now? *Crime and Delinquency, 43*, 345–357.

Zhao, J. S., Scheider, M. C., & Thurman, Q. T. (2002). Funding community policing to reduce crime: Have COPS grants made a difference? *Criminology and Public Policy, 2*, 7–32.

Zimring, F. E. (2008). *The great American crime decline*. New York: Oxford University Press.

COURT CASES CITED

Arizona v. Evans, 514 U.S. 1 (1995).

Brown v. Board of Education, 347 U.S. 483 (1954).

Brown v. Mississippi, 297 U.S. 278 (1936).

Duckworth v. Eagan, 492 U.S. 195 (1989).

Gideon v. Wainwright, 372 U.S. 335 (1963).

Griswold v. Connecticut, 381 U.S. 479 (1965).

Mapp v. Ohio, 367 U.S. 643 (1961).

Massachusetts v. Sheppard, 468 U.S. 981 (1984).

Miranda v. Arizona, 382 U.S. 436 (1966).

New York v. Quarles, 467 U.S. 649 (1984).

Nix v. Williams, 467 U.S. 431 (1984).

Pennsylvania v. Nelson, 350 U.S. 497 (1956).

Pennsylvania v. Muniz, 496 U.S. 582 (1990).

Reynolds v. Sims, 377 U.S. 533 (1964)

Roth v. United States, 354 U.S. 476 (1957).

Terry v. Ohio, 392 U.S. 1 (1968).

United States v. Sokolow, 490 U.S. 1 (1989).

Watkins v. United States, 354 U.S. 178 (1957).

Weeks v. The United States, 232 U.S. 383 (1914).

Index

About the Author

Jonathon A. Cooper is an assistant professor of criminology and criminal justice at Indiana University of Pennsylvania, where he also directs the Criminology Advising Center. His interest in the history of policing, and how that history matters for contemporary law enforcement, began in 2004 after taking a policing course from Dr. Andrew Giacomazzi at Boise State University, and was enriched by his graduate education at Arizona State University, where he earned his doctorate in criminology and criminal justice. He and his family currently live in Indiana, Pennsylvania.